DOLORES HUERTA STANDS STRONG

DOLORES HUERTA STANDS STRONG

THE WOMAN WHO DEMANDED JUSTICE

Marlene Targ Brill

BIOGRAPHIES FOR YOUNG READERS

Ohio University Press

Athens

Ohio University Press, Athens, Ohio 45701
ohioswallow.com
© 2018 by Marlene Targ Brill

To obtain permission to quote, reprint, or otherwise reproduce or distribute
material from Ohio University Press publications, please contact our rights
and permissions department at (740) 593-1154 or (740) 593-4536 (fax).

Printed in the United States of America
Ohio University Press books are printed on acid-free paper ⊗™

28 27 26 25 24 23 22 21 20 19 18   5 4 3 2 1

Frontispiece: Dolores Huerta in a hand-knit sweater vest displaying
the UFW eagle. *UFW Collection, 199*

All photos from the UFW Collection are used by permission of the
Walter P. Reuther Library, Archives of Labor and Urban Affairs,
Wayne State University

Hardcover ISBN: 978-0-8214-2329-5
Paperback ISBN: 978-0-8214-2330-1
Electronic ISBN: 978-0-8214-4643-0

Library of Congress Cataloging in Publication Data available upon request.

Contents

Author's Note

GROWING UP in the 1960s was often confusing. Television and newspaper reports switched from good to bad, sometimes within hours—sort of like today. But I was still too young to make sense of a world beyond my immediate community, especially one that seemed so topsy-turvy.

On the surface, the decade shouted, "Fun!" Teens celebrated peace, love, and rock and roll. Often when those peace-and-love people danced in the streets, adults registered shock or disapproval. But the economy was strong, and people had money to spend. The time seemed right for experimenting.

When the decade began, most kids looked buttoned down and acted within the assumed rules of the day. Girls dressed in bobby sox and skirts and wore their hair in ponytails or pixie cuts. Boys sported pants and loafers and favored crewcuts or slicked-back hairstyles. By the late 1960s, many girls had switched to mod tunics, miniskirts, and tie-dyed or peasant tops. Conservative clothing in solids and plaids evolved into multicolored and wildly tailored garments that showed considerably more skin. Almost everyone wore jeans and sneakers, something out of the question years earlier. Both boys and girls grew their hair long, and males wore long, sculpted sideburns, too.

A war was raging in Vietnam. But that was far away. At home, music and the arts championed the idea that we should all try to get along. Then war would end. Life would become less angry and complicated. Everything would be groovy, a popular term at the time.

In 1960, Americans elected their youngest president to date. At age forty-four, John Kennedy was smart and handsome, full of new ideas.

He had the personality to convince citizens to put his ideas into action. At his 1961 inauguration, he challenged the nation to "ask not what your country will do for you—ask what you can do for your country." That simple statement dared me to think about my future and what it might bring.

One of President Kennedy's most popular achievements was the launch of a space program. He hoped to put a man on the moon. At first, I thought it was crazy talk. Still, it was a positive sign in a world of upheaval. That scientific triumph, which eventually took place in 1969, raised hopes of great possibilities for the future—maybe my future. I could dream.

Besides good vibes, the decade brought radical change to nearly every segment of the population. Young people marched for civil rights for women, Native Americans, people with disabilities, and African Americans. I felt forced to think about life in a different way. Why were certain people treated as harshly as they were? Who decided that only men could obtain credit cards and bank loans? What law said that women needed to marry and raise families to be fulfilled? Why were people with disabilities locked in institutions and Native Americans forced onto barren reservations? Moreover, why were African Americans and other minorities treated as second-class citizens?

I lived in a northern Midwestern state. I had trouble understanding why southern towns forced black people to attend separate schools, drink from separate water fountains, and enter theaters by separate entrances from whites. Newscasts showed police beating and letting loose attack dogs on these citizens for nothing more than their marching to attain equal rights. I knew this wasn't fair.

I had no idea at the time that other groups were experiencing much the same treatment, just because they were Latinos, immigrants, or other minorities. I wondered what I could do to change these injustices. I guess the oppressed families experiencing those injustices wondered, too. Many joined **sit-ins, boycotts**, and marches to protest unfair treatment; to have their voices heard; and to enact change at all levels of society. Now that I look back, these wonderings led to my becoming an author. I wanted to give voice to the voiceless and unrecognized.

During the 1960s another group, farmworkers, protested against unfair treatment. I never really considered how my food got to the dinner table. I knew that fruits and vegetables were planted, picked, packaged, then sent to markets in big cities, like the one in which I lived. But I never thought about the lives of the farmworkers who made all this happen. I had no idea that the workers who picked my food received extremely low wages. I had no idea that the farm owners abused these workers with terrible living conditions and long workdays. I had no idea that entire families, including children who should have been in school, picked my fruits and vegetables in order to earn enough to *buy* their own food—the same food that they were picking.

I knew little about the structure of this food chain—until I saw the signs. People were marching everywhere—in front of stores, in nearby streets. Many held signs describing those unfair work conditions. Marchers urged shoppers to stop buying table grapes. On different occasions, they pleaded with shoppers to avoid buying lettuce. Just out of college and full of a desire to right society's wrongs, I wanted to support the workers who were producing my food. But there were so many products I was told not to purchase. Which ones should or shouldn't I buy to help the workers? I was confused.

One voice rose above the noise to clarify the issues. That voice belonged to Dolores Huerta, and she appeared on media often to talk about the grape **strike**. I saw her on news shows. I heard her in radio interviews. This petite, dark-haired **Chicana** carried the torch for farmworkers and anyone else treated unjustly.

What impressed me about her rapid-fire explanations was her hopeful attitude. No matter how badly the fieldworkers were treated, how harsh their lives were, she always saw possibilities rather than problems. Failure was not an option. Through her organizing skills and her ability to clearly explain what took place in the fields, she gave voice to the voiceless. She taught average people like me to speak up, to band together, to join the fight to make a difference.

I wanted to know more about this strong-willed woman. As I read about her, I wondered why she gave up so much of her life to help people she didn't know. I wanted to know how she came to the causes she championed. Over the years, Dolores also campaigned on behalf of women and other minorities. What gave her the courage to stand strong and demand justice from rich growers, large corporations, politicians, and police?

DOLORES
HUERTA
STANDS
STRONG

ONE

HARVESTING THE FRUITS OF LABOR

Symbol of Justice

P RESIDENT BARACK OBAMA is one person on a long list of admirers who agree with Dolores Huerta's calls for justice. On May 29, 2012, Dolores Clara Fernández Huerta looked on as the president introduced rows of award winners at a special ceremony. Her eyes sparkled. What would the president say about her? She sat up straight. She looked regal dressed in a formal turquoise suit, unlike the work jeans and T-shirts that she usually wore. Today, she dressed like the honored White House guest she was.

Dolores smiled sweetly. The eighty-two-year-old woman appeared calm. But inside, her heart must have leaped with excitement and pride. She'd received plenty of honors over the past few years. But this one came from a president who believed—as she did—in the power of community organizing.

Dolores was one of thirteen honorees: former secretary of state Madeleine Albright, Associate Supreme Court Justice John Paul Stevens, musician Bob Dylan, author Toni Morrison, physician and scientist William Foege, astronaut John Glenn, former Israeli president Shimon Peres, women's basketball coach Pat Summitt, attorney and civil rights activist John Doar, Girls Scouts founder Juliette Gordon Low, World War II Polish resistance leader Jan Karski, and sociologist and human rights activist Gordon Hirabayashi. Here she sat, among the other surviving awardees. What a journey she had made to get to this place of honor.

Dolores had spent a lifetime fighting for the rights of anyone treated unfairly—people who looked, acted, thought, or felt differently from how others believed they should. Dolores had never done it for the recognition. She fought so that other people could live better lives because of the work that she helped to accomplish. And here she was, about to receive the 2012 **Presidential Medal of Freedom**, the highest civilian honor that the United States bestows.

When her turn came, President Obama introduced Dolores and listed some of her achievements. He recalled how in 1955 she had left her career as a schoolteacher without thought of how little she was about to earn. Back then, she was a single mother of seven. But she felt called upon to quit teaching in order to improve her students' lives. She figured she could help her students more by organizing their poor farmworker families to fight for better living and working conditions than by trying to force those young, hungry, and exhausted students to learn.

Dolores wanted community members to stand up for themselves. She decided that she would lead them, be their voice. She pushed the fruit and vegetable growers who hired farmworkers to pay those workers a fair wage, to treat them with respect, and to stop spraying the fields with **pesticides** while they worked.

Dolores was a tiny woman, about five feet tall, but she was mighty. Many called her fearless. She was driven by the idea that change could happen if individuals banded together. She, like the president, believed that a group that speaks with one voice can achieve more than individuals. President Obama recounted how, with no experience in labor negotiations, Dolores "helped lead a worldwide grape boycott that forced

2

President Barack Obama awarding Dolores Huerta the Presidential Medal of Freedom

Photo: Rena Schild/Shutterstock

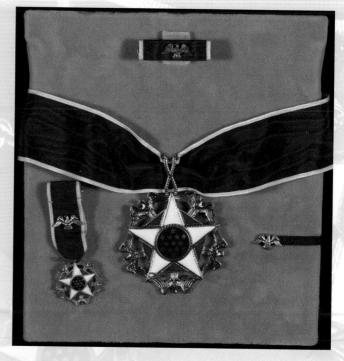

The Presidential Medal of Freedom displays the red, white, and blue presidential seal. The thirteen gold stars represent the thirteen original colonies and are surrounded by gold eagles.

growers to agree to some of the country's first farm worker contracts. And ever since, she has fought to give more people a seat at the table."[1]

Then Obama thanked Dolores for letting him use her slogan, "Sí Se Puede"—"Yes, We Can"—when he ran for president. He joked about how he never wanted to cross her by using the slogan, the words that advertised her causes, without permission. *She was that tough.* Dolores smiled.

After Obama fastened the Presidential Medal of Freedom around Dolores's neck, he bent over and hugged her. Everyone in the room clapped. Dolores beamed.

Dolores had been through a lot over the years—beatings, jail. She had endured time away from her children, miles of marches, and end-

THE PRESIDENTIAL MEDAL OF FREEDOM

ON JULY 6, 1945, President Harry S. Truman signed an executive order that established the Medal of Freedom to honor civilians who had contributed notable service during World War II. President John F. Kennedy renamed the award the Presidential Medal of Freedom in 1963. He expanded the scope of the award to include anyone who contributed extensively to public security, world peace, or cultural or other activities. The award was for individuals who made a difference for others, whatever their field of accomplishment.

While some formal awards are given often—to foreign heads of state or for military achievements—only a few people receive the Presidential Medal of Freedom. An executive order calls for the awards to be offered yearly, but that hasn't always happened. Although the president may take suggestions for honorees, the ultimate decision belongs to the president. Of the 550 recipients of the Presidential Medal of Freedom, Dolores was only the second woman of Mexican descent to receive this honor.

less travel. Her family members and neighbors had been treated without respect. She had spent long hours making speeches and protesting in front of companies and government buildings. But over the years, the hard work of battling injustice and her passion for what she believed in had attracted considerable attention. Her notoriety eventually brought many awards, including honorary degrees from universities. Numerous elementary and high schools had been renamed after her. Now President Obama had chosen to honor her with the highest award any American civilian could receive.

To Dolores, however, the greatest prize was the success she had achieved in encouraging others toward a better life. After the ceremony Dolores said, "My most memorable advice from my mother was: 'When you see people who need help, you should help them. You shouldn't wait for people to ask.' When I learned organizing skills, I had an obligation to teach people to come together to fight for what they need."[2]

DID YOU KNOW?

Chicano/Chicana, Latino/Latina, Mexican American, or Hispanic? Many people get confused about which term to use to describe people in the United States who are of Spanish-speaking descent—and about whether such labeling is necessary at all. Definitions and how they are received vary, depending on what sources are consulted. "Chicano" refers to someone of Mexican origin who was born in the United States, like Dolores. While some people view the term negatively, because it was first used as an insult, others take pride in the term, noting the work of the Chicano Movement, or La Causa, for its fight for civil rights and better treatment of its people. "Latino" refers to geographical origins, particularly of those countries that were under Roman rule long ago. "Hispanic" usually refers to immigrants from countries that speak Spanish, including Mexico and many other places in Central America, South America, and the Caribbean islands. Both "Latino" and "Hispanic" bother some people, too. And to some, "Mexican American" implies a split identity. More often, someone whose native language is Spanish prefers to be identified by their country of origin, such as Mexican or Peruvian, rather than to be lumped under one vast regional or ethnic term.

TWO

TILLING THE SOIL

Born to Speak Out

B OTH PARENTS OF Dolores Fernández Huerta were born in the United States but with different family backgrounds. Her father, Juan Fernández, came from Dawson, a mining town in the mountains of northern New Mexico. Juan's parents had arrived from Mexico not long before he was born. On Dolores's mother's side, the family's roots in the area extended back to the 1600s.

Both families lived and worked in the New Mexico region. There Alicia, Dolores's mother, met Juan. Their only daughter was born on April 10, 1930. The young couple named the baby Dolores, which means "pain" or "suffering" in Spanish. After she married, Dolores took the last name Huerta, which means "garden" or "orchard." Together, these names fit her well. Dolores's future would be tied to the land and the people who toiled to produce its crops. Almost seventy years later, in his speech honoring Dolores with the Eleanor Roosevelt Award for Human Rights, President Bill Clinton stated, "But if Dolores Huerta has her way, her name will be the only sorrowful orchard left in America."[1]

Dolores, her older brother, Juan, and her younger brother, Marshall, were all born in Dawson. Their father and other relatives mined coal in that small town of about nine thousand people. Dolores's birth came during the **Great Depression**, a national economic downturn that strained the ability of many families to earn a living. Between 1929 and 1939, this recession worsened, becoming the deepest and longest financial depression in the western world. Factories, businesses, and mines closed, leaving several million workers without jobs—including Juan.

To supplement the family's reduced income, Juan picked vegetables. As family finances worsened, Juan migrated to Wyoming and Nebraska, as did many other poor workers. They followed the harvests and picked different crops as they ripened.

There seemed no end in sight for the poor economy, so the entire family packed up and followed Juan as he moved from place to place. They lived in tarpaper shacks, learning firsthand how difficult the life of a poor farmworker family could be. For the first time, they faced the sting of **racism**, being targeted because they were Mexican Americans.

Juan was smart and hard working, and he was growing angrier about their situation. Poor living and working conditions and related daily hardships strained the relationship between Juan and Alicia. They divorced when Dolores was about five years old.

Alicia eventually moved her children to Stockton, California, where she had other family. The port of Stockton sat alongside rich farmland in the north-central San Joaquin Valley. Originally a Native American settlement, then land owned by Mexico, Stockton transformed into a commercial center after the discovery of gold in 1848. Gold seekers arrived from every continent, creating a town with a very mixed population. When the gold fever subsided, the region's economy shifted to agriculture. After Chinese immigrants helped lay train tracks connecting Stockton to the rest of the state and the country, it became an important transportation hub for agricultural products. Several communities of farmworkers developed.

A farmworker in the open fields
UFW Collection, 335

LIFE AS A FARMWORKER

Picking fruits and vegetables could be brutal work. Days started at sunup when workers boarded rickety buses to travel into the fields. Pickers stayed in the fields until sundown, working under a blistering sun with few breaks and little water. Sometimes, foremen provided only a single soda can of water for an entire truckload of workers to drink. Once the can was emptied, it was not refilled. Growers rarely provided toilets or shelter from the sun. Workers were allowed no privacy, and they had nowhere to go. They were trapped in the middle of fields that sometimes stretched for twenty miles.

Growers often preferred to hire immigrants. Being new to the United States, their understanding of English was poor, so they were unable to organize or complain. In addition, many of these workers were in the country illegally and could lose their jobs and be **deported** if they were discovered. Bosses would use this threat to keep their crews in line.[2]

People had to work quickly to earn a decent day's wage, which was usually based on the weight or number of fruits or vegetables picked. Because dishonest farm owners could keep their wage records secret, workers often received less pay than they deserved. Without access to records, workers would have difficulty proving their loss, especially if they didn't speak English very well.

To pick low-growing crops, like strawberries, workers had to bend over, kneel, and sometimes crawl from plant to plant. If plants required digging, short-handled hoes forced workers to stoop down, which made the task even more backbreaking. Farmworkers became as physically fit as athletes or dancers, but the brutal picking speed and constant bending over could make farmworkers aged thirty look like they were forty.[3]

As an adult, Dolores told journalist Studs Terkel that she believed this system of degrading workers affected them more than the backbreaking labor itself. Some growers thought that their workers were inferior and humiliated them. Others were greedy or simply indifferent to what foremen did. "No one should have to endure this deliberate subhuman treatment designed to keep farmworker families down," Dolores said. "This kind of treatment kills the spirit."[4]

GROWING UP IN FARM COUNTRY

Dolores's widowed grandfather, Herculana Chávez, helped watch Alicia's children so she could find work. Herculana became an important figure in Dolores's life. He encouraged his smart, chatty granddaughter, giving her the nickname "seven tongues" because she talked so much.[5] Dolores learned early that speaking her mind and arguing about things that were important were good skills to cultivate.

Even with family to help her, Alicia found supporting her children difficult during the long depression. She needed to be especially clever and hardworking. She took two jobs just to put enough food on the

Farmworkers using short-handled hoes to harvest crops
UFW Collection, 244

table and build a small savings. She waited tables during the day and worked in a cannery by night. "My mother had a good head for business," Dolores remembered later, "so she worked a couple of jobs and managed to open up a small business."[6]

Alicia treated her sons and daughter equally. She never singled out Dolores to do what was considered "women's work," like washing dishes, ironing clothes, or waiting on the boys. Dolores grew up believing that a woman's voice was just as important as a man's.

When Juan and Marshall grew old enough, they picked tomatoes on nearby farms. But here Alicia drew the line with her daughter. Alicia never allowed Dolores to work in the fields. She did not want her daughter to experience the hardships of farm labor and indecent treatment by foremen. When Dolores was a teenager, Alicia permitted her to work in the packing sheds, where she learned about the difficult labor involved in packaging fruits and vegetables, but Dolores never endured the brutal fieldwork. Later, Dolores would tease that her mother had stunted her education by not giving her experience as a field laborer.[7]

Alicia's determination and solid business sense earned her enough savings to buy a little lunch counter. As the restaurant prospered, she expanded to a bigger restaurant. After marrying her second husband, James Richards, Alicia bought a small hotel in Stockton. Dolores soon had a half-sister.

WATCHING AND LEARNING

Alicia always welcomed working-class people and farm laborers, or *campesinos,* who came from the poor area near the hotel. She offered lodging to low-wage workers for one dollar a room, a small amount even in the 1930s. Sometimes she asked for no fee at all. Alicia understood the hardships that poor people endured. Dolores saw how her mother treated all her boarders with compassion and respect; she watched her mother become an involved and outspoken leader in civic organizations and the church.

Dolores's neighborhood was more diverse than many other farm communities at the time. Her family's home was near a Filipino pool hall and a Mexican-owned drugstore and bakery. Jewish families lived nearby. Dolores attended grade school with blacks, whites, Native Americans, and Italians, in addition to Mexican Americans. Her best friend came from a Chinese and Buddhist home, and they shared their family traditions. Dolores later credited the time in this *barrio,* or neighborhood, with teaching her to appreciate individual differences among people.

Together with her classmates, Dolores joined the Girl Scouts, a group where everyone was made to feel special. As her mother's income increased, she encouraged Dolores and her brothers to take violin, piano, and dance lessons and to sing in the church choir. They joined a local youth organization. Dolores rarely knew discrimination among her classmates or from the school staff. Teachers were strict; they treated every student sternly. Dolores and her friends thought they were all mean.

A DIFFERENT KIND OF EDUCATION

When Dolores reached high school, however, she faced a different, more **segregated** environment. Rich students from the north side of town and poor teens from the south and east sides were thrown together. Some wealthier students bullied those from homes with less money to spare for the latest clothes and extra items. Minority teens were often excluded from high school activities. Many school social clubs charged fees for dances, knowing poor students could never afford to attend.

Although Dolores worked hard and received good grades for the most part, she also faced discrimination from teachers who routinely gave lower grades to Mexican American students. In one class, Dolores received an A on all her papers throughout the year, yet her teacher gave her a final grade of C. "I used to be able to write really nice, poetry and everything," Dolores wrote later. "But the teacher told me at the end of the year that she couldn't give me an A because she knew that somebody was writing my papers for me. That really discouraged me, because I used to stay up all night and think, and try to make every paper different, and try to put words in there that I thought were nice. It kind of crushed me. I was frustrated. You're trying to go to school and yet you see all of these injustices."[8]

Although Dolores won a contest for selling the most **war bonds,** she did not receive the trophy. Sponsors figured a Mexican girl could never have achieved so many sales. She began to feel like an outsider. Dolores believed later that she was treated differently because she was "poor, Mexican American, and a girl."[9]

Alicia advised her bright daughter to just be herself. Alicia's support helped Dolores deal with the slights she felt from not being accepted. Dolores stayed active in various groups throughout high school.

She became a majorette. She helped start other social activities, including a teen center. Then the police closed the center down because some citizens objected to white girls and boys mixing with people of color. Always determined, Dolores formed another group. The police closed that one, too.

When Dolores was fifteen, attackers beat and stripped her brother Marshall at a party he attended to celebrate the end of World War II. The thugs said the reason for the attack involved what her brother wore —a **zoot suit**. Zoot suits, which included high-waisted, wide-legged, tight-cuffed trousers and a long coat with wide lapels and wide padded shoulders, were popular with Chicano, African American, Filipino, and Italian men during the 1940s. The attack on Marshall was about race, not clothes.

Dolores saw discrimination and unjust treatment firsthand, but she learned from these experiences and tried to rise above them. Her teen years taught her the power of bringing people together, as she had with the teen center, to fight discrimination.

DID YOU KNOW?

During the 1940s, when Dolores was growing up, many communities followed written and unwritten rules to keep people of different races separate from each other. Certain neighborhoods banned Latinos, Jews, African Americans, and Asians from schools, libraries, and stores in areas dominated by whites. Some housing developments required buyers to sign whites-only property contracts. Businesses in southern towns and northern cities alike posted signs to indicate separate water fountains, restrooms, and seating in theaters. Interstate trains declared whites-only dining cars. In 1960, when President Barack Obama's white mother and African father married, half the states in the country still banned marriages between people of different races.

THREE

FERTILIZING THE SOIL

The Making of an Organizer

A s a young girl and teenager, Dolores rarely conformed to other people's standards. Instead, she followed the path she believed was right, often going against her community's strict traditional rules for what girls and women could or could not do. She helped in her mother's grocery store, restaurant, and hotel together with her brothers. After high school graduation, she pursued an education at Stockton Junior College, something her mother encouraged. This was an unusual direction for a Mexican American teen in the 1940s, particularly a girl.

Discrimination and poverty forced most of her classmates from elementary school to drop out when they reached high school. This thought never occurred to Dolores; her family placed a high value on education. Because of her family's support, she never minded being the only Chicana in her college classes. She often surprised classmates by her willingness to speak her mind during discussions.

When Dolores turned seventeen, Alicia took her to Mexico City. This was her first trip to a Mexican community outside the United

States. The experience increased her pride in her Mexican heritage. It also opened her eyes to the amount of discrimination Chicanas faced at home.

Back in California, her frustration about not being accepted pushed her to join Chicano organizations. These groups mainly held dances and fiestas. Music and special foods were an important part of her Mexican heritage, but Dolores wanted action—and change. Although injustices that she witnessed began to gnaw at her, she found no outlet for these feelings.

Dolores did follow custom in one area. During college, she took a break from classes to marry a high school boyfriend, Ralph Head, just before her twentieth birthday. Within a short time, they had two daughters, Celeste and Lori. But the marriage did not last long. After the divorce, Dolores and her daughters moved in with Alicia. As an independent single mother herself, Alicia understood the difficulties Dolores faced. She helped support the small family with money and encouragement. Both allowed Dolores to continue college and receive an associate of arts degree.

After college, Dolores tried a variety of jobs. She worked at the naval supply base in Stockton as the commander's secretary. She also handled records for the sheriff's office. Each job taught her practical business skills, but both left her unfulfilled. So Dolores returned to the University of the Pacific to earn a teaching certificate.

Dolores enjoyed teaching children. She understood how important education was to getting ahead in life. But she grew frustrated, knowing how difficult it was for her students to learn. Her class included children from a mix of ethnic backgrounds, but all were poor. Many students came from farmworker families. They arrived at school in tattered clothes and shoes or no shoes at all. Some were so undernourished that bony limbs poked from their thin shirts. Students told her how they lived with large families in tiny, rundown shacks—or even in cars—making sleeping difficult. Her students came to school tired and hungry, if they came at all. These parents counted on their children to help earn money so that the family could eat. Although many students tried to attend when they could be spared from working in the fields, without time to study or enough food to nourish their bodies and minds, how could they possibly learn and progress?

Dolores asked the principal about getting her students free lunch and milk. He responded without feeling, wrongly assuming that these children came from families with parents who didn't care about their kids—parents who drank away their earnings. If these students needed free lunches, he felt, their parents should go to the **welfare** department and beg. The principal never considered the long hours these parents worked under terrible conditions to earn so little.

TIME FOR CHANGE

After talking with the principal, Dolores decided the best way to help her students was to help their parents gain better working conditions. To do that, she joined the new Stockton branch of the Community Service Organization (CSO). Newly formed by a man named Fred Ross, the CSO hoped to become a Mexican American self-help association.

Fred Ross had arrived from Los Angeles with a passion for battling injustice. He believed that an activist's job was to light a flame under people who could work for change within their own community. His way of spreading his message was to go from door to door and to hold house meetings, building a movement of people from the bottom up, like grass from roots.[1] He claimed, "If we got together, we could register voters, elect Spanish-speaking representatives, and turn everything around."[2] Fred talked about how the CSO had started health clinics in San Jose and had integrated schools that previously were separated into all-Mexican, all-black, or all-white classes. He showed Dolores pictures of crowds of one hundred to two hundred people attending CSO meetings. And he told her of the skills and dedication of another CSO worker, César Chávez.

Left to right: César Chávez, Fred Ross, Luis Valdez, Dolores Huerta
UFW Collection, 288

At first Dolores refused to believe Fred. Being a careful person, she used her connections at the sheriff's office to check out his background with the Federal Bureau of Investigation (FBI). As she learned more about him, Dolores came to understand what Fred was trying to accomplish and realized that he wanted to help the same people she did. She thought long and hard about leaving teaching with two children at home. Ultimately, Dolores made that gutsy move. She quit her teaching job to spend more time working with the CSO.

"When I made the decision to quit teaching, it took a lot of faith," Dolores recalled later. "After I had made that decision, the very next morning, I woke up to find that someone had left a box of groceries on my porch."[3] Dolores took this as a sign that she had made the right choice.

Living conditions in a farm labor camp
UFW Collection, 7118

One mission of the CSO was to increase political power in Spanish-speaking communities. To do that, adults needed to understand that their votes counted. Fred gave Dolores a job registering people to vote. Going door to door, she visited the families of many former students. What she saw saddened her. Dolores found the children living in run-down dwellings with dirt floors. Many lacked plumbing, having no running water to wash clothes and only outhouses for toilets. Women cooked on single burners because they had no stoves or ovens. Some growers provided their workers with shacks but surrounded those shacks with barbed wire.

Such terrible living arrangements fueled Dolores's passion for change. She became a tireless worker for the CSO, running education and community programs. Along the way, Fred trained her in the best ways of inspiring others to help themselves. One way was to vote. Registering people to vote benefited both Dolores and those she registered. As she became emboldened, Dolores began to achieve small successes. She went to police departments and appealed for an end to needless searches and other harassments of Latinos without cause. She moved local officials to improve neighborhood services.

TWO SOULMATES MEET

During a 1960 voter drive that registered 150,000 people, Dolores met César Chávez, the CSO worker Fred Ross had spoken of earlier. Hearing César address a gathering, Dolores found him inspiring. As she listened to more of his speeches, she was drawn to his soft-spoken but steady presence. César, in turn, liked how Dolores got results when she attacked a project. This one-hundred-pound, five-foot-tall woman with black hair and striking features projected intelligence and determination. She spoke her mind in short, easy-to-follow messages without worrying what others thought. Another plus was her background. César had spent his entire life traveling from farm field to farm field, never having one home. Dolores had grown up living in one community, in a city. She had visited other regions and met different types of people, widening her perspectives.

César suggested that the CSO hire Dolores as a full-time activist, which Fred did. Her job was to convince lawmakers to vote the CSO way. She produced such positive results that Fred offered her the opportunity to be the voice of the CSO. He sent Dolores to Sacramento, the state capital, to **lobby** legislators to enact laws that would benefit poor and immigrant workers.

Together, César and Dolores fought for **pensions** for noncitizens. Pensions would give older and disabled workers income to retire, something previously unavailable to workers in the fields. The two pushed lawmakers to include farmworkers in a welfare bill that offered money to parents so they could stay home to care for their young children. The two advocated for **disability insurance** to guarantee income for

César with his car called "Huelga," or "Strike" in English
UFW Collection, 228

injured or sick farmworkers who were unable to work. Dolores and César championed the cause of allowing Latino immigrants to take their driver's license exam in Spanish. And they urged an end to the **Bracero Program.**

THE BRACERO PROGRAM

On August 4, 1942, the United States and Mexican governments negotiated an agreement, officially known as the Mexican Farm Labor Program, more commonly referred to as the Bracero Program. (*Bracero* is Spanish for a person who works with their hands, a manual laborer.) The program was designed to fill the shortages of agricultural laborers that had developed during World War II because so many citizens were enlisting in the military. Under its terms, Mexican migrant workers were granted temporary contracts for work on farms in the United States. They were promised fair living and working conditions— affordable food and adequate, free, and sanitary housing, plus a minimum wage of thirty cents an hour. They were also guaranteed access without discrimination to *gringo*, or white, areas surrounding the farms.

21

These promises of fair treatment were soon broken. Administrators from both countries discovered the potential for huge profits—at the workers' expense. Mexican officials took bribes to allow many more immigrants, even young children, to cross the border illegally. U.S. labor inspectors received money to look the other way when employers failed to provide braceros fair or equal treatment.

Under the agreement, braceros could not bargain for better wages. If they complained, their bosses simply shipped them back to Mexico. By the 1950s, farm owners preferred to hire braceros rather than U.S. citizens. Because the braceros earned less than U.S. workers, more money was left for the owners.

Workers' organizations and church groups criticized the program. As protests increased, the federal government gradually passed laws to protect braceros, but those laws weren't enough. It took twenty-two years and numerous protesters, including Dolores Huerta and César Chávez, before the Bracero Program officially ended in 1964.

While working with the CSO, Dolores met and married her second husband, Ventura Huerta. Their marriage produced five children: Fidel, Emilio, Vincent, Alicia, and Angela. At first, the two shared a commitment to community activities. But Ventura had other ideas about what a wife's role should be. He wanted someone who acted more like a traditional mother, someone who stayed home with their children and kept house for her husband. This was not Dolores's plan. Their differences eventually led to a bitter divorce.

Meanwhile, Dolores continued to display boundless energy for improving the lives of farmworkers. She joined an agricultural group founded by a local priest, which soon became part of the Agricultural Workers Organizing Committee (AWOC). Dolores served as treasurer.

As time passed, however, Dolores felt that the AWOC wasn't really helping farmworkers. Neither the AWOC nor the CSO wanted to organize a **union** specifically for fieldworkers. The creation of a farmworkers union became the main goal for Dolores and her activist soulmate, César Chávez.

One day, César invited Dolores to his house. He said, "You know, farmworkers are never going to have a union unless you and I start it."[4] Dolores thought it was a joke and laughed. But César explained that he was dead serious. Farmworkers needed to band together to represent themselves in a union of their own. Such a union could represent the interests of all its members through **collective bargaining,** negotiations with their employers over wages and working conditions. The process proved to be a huge step forward for farmworkers.

At the time, Dolores had six children with a seventh on the way. She was a single mother with a low-paying job. But a farmworkers union was her dream, as well as César's. The two had no idea what they were getting into—or the resistance they would encounter.

DID YOU KNOW?

When Dolores began organizing, many people assumed that there was only one way that work should be divided between men and women. Men provided income for their families. Women kept the house and cared for children— unless the family was poor. Then, women worked alongside their husbands. They were, however, still responsible for taking care of the home, including serving their husbands. In Chicano culture, this sense of male pride had a name: *machismo.* In Mexico, the term originally referred to someone who was educated and a role model. But over time, the meaning changed. Men assumed that they were superior to women, that they were protectors of the weaker sex, and that they always should have the final word. When Dolores first joined the CSO, she was told, "Farm labor organizing was no place for a woman." "So," she said, "I kind of worked undercover, doing the work through my husband and my brother."[5] Instead of backing down, Dolores took her already smart and outspoken style and made it even bolder.

FOUR

PLANTING THE SEEDS

Building La Causa

D OLORES AND CÉSAR began their new project with hope and a fierce desire for change. But first, they had to discover what the farmworkers themselves wanted.

They started by preparing leaflets that explained their idea of taking action. César borrowed a hand-cranked **mimeograph** machine to print them, and Dolores enlisted her children to deliver them—door to door and store to store. They started in Sacramento and headed north through California's Central Valley. César and his family moved southward toward Modesto. Then Dolores and César followed up, going to each individual home. They answered questions and asked people to support their efforts.

Once Dolores and César knew that enough workers were in favor of forming a union, they held a large meeting, or convention. The new organization, the National Farm Workers Association (NFWA), held its first meeting in a deserted theater in Fresno, California, on September 30, 1962. The group's first job was to elect officers and delegates to represent the different communities.

Dolores signing up workers for the new union
UFW Collection, 238

Dolores did not want to be an officer, but César disagreed. "You have to be an officer," he told Dolores. "The people who actually do the work are going to run this union."[1] That was their **grassroots** philosophy: the union must belong to its members. Dolores finally agreed and was elected as one of two vice presidents. César became president.

Dolores and César shared their vision with the 150 delegates and their families who attended. They envisioned a strong association that bargained with growers to secure higher wages and better living and working conditions for all its members. Dolores and César wanted guarantees from owners that workers could return to the same farms each year. With promises of steady work, workers could lay down roots, build a community, and send their children to the same schools each season, just like other families. Union leaders called for an end to spraying unhealthy chemicals on the crops while workers labored in the fields;

they asked for health insurance for workers who got sick. Delegates also urged an end to the Bracero Program that allowed growers to pay immigrants less than other fieldworkers and to treat them poorly.

César emphasized that these goals should be achieved peacefully. He talked about the civil rights movement for African Americans that was spreading throughout the country and about Reverend Martin Luther King Jr.'s plea for nonviolence. But how could the workers achieve their goals by peaceful means? The answer was simple: by using the power of the strike. In a strike, he explained, all members of a union stop working at the same time. Without farmworkers, how would owners get their crops picked, packed, and sent to market? How would they make money if the fruits and vegetables remained lying in the fields?

During the convention, members voted to adopt "Viva La Causa!" (Long Live the Cause!) as their motto. They voted that each member would pay monthly dues of $3.50 to support the work of the union. This seemed a small amount, but it reflected how little farmworkers earned.

Before closing the meeting, César unveiled a union flag intended to unite union members. César chose a black eagle, drawn with sharp, straight lines, on a white circle with a red background. Black represented the dark situation that workers endured in the fields. The white circle shone as a symbol of hope. The red background highlighted the sweat and "sacrifice that the Association and its members will have to contribute to gain justice for the farmworkers."[2] The membership voted to accept the flag as the association's official symbol.

Dolores played a strong decision-making role in the union leadership. She contributed to strategy, organization, and direction, helping shape the NFWA. She never worried about criticism for being a woman handling what many people thought of as a man's job. She was bold, smart, and unafraid of anyone. Once workers felt her passion and motivation, they accepted her as a leader. "Anyone who can do the job is welcome to come in and share the suffering," Dolores wrote.[3]

Although César and many union leaders emphasized equal rights for women, others held on to outdated views about a woman's place in

The Filipino United Farm Workers Union picketing to support the UFW
UFW Collection, 225

society. Dolores, with her usual clever and direct style, confronted the discrimination head-on. "The men would come out and say their stupid little jokes about women," she remembered. "So I started keeping a record. At the end of the meeting, I'd say, 'During the course of this meeting you men have made fifty-eight sexist remarks.' Pretty soon I got them down to twenty-five, then ten, and then five."[4]

FAMILY LIFE WHILE BUILDING A UNION

César decided that the union's central office should be in Delano, California, and he suggested that Dolores move her family nearby. Dolores worried about how she could earn enough to feed her children, but César assured her that anyone who worked for La Causa would never starve. The people would never let that happen.

ORGANIZING FARM LABOR
IN THE UNITED STATES

DURING THE early twentieth century, the need for factories to process goods expanded alongside population growth. As the number of un-skilled factory jobs increased, attempts to organize workers for higher wages and better working conditions quickly emerged. With the grow-ing need to feed these many new workers, farmworkers called for unions of their own.

The first wave of union activity dedicated to farm labor began in 1905 with the formation of the Industrial Workers of the World (IWW). By 1913, California had become a hotbed of IWW protest strikes to improve farmworker conditions. Growers fought the strikes with crackdowns on organizers. National attention to these battles led to the first union established in the United States for farmworkers only—the Agricultural Workers Organization. The entry of the country into World War I led to the decline of unions as all attention turned to the war effort.

At first, some of her children stayed with relatives. Others lived with her and the Chávez family. When a little more money became available, Dolores moved into her own home. Her older children watched the younger ones. They often accompanied their mother to speeches and marches; they joined her in knocking on doors. She packed the kids in the car at night and on weekends to travel between migrant labor camps, and she nursed her young baby while on the road. Her children never complained. They knew that their mother was working for an important cause: justice.

Fighting for important causes was in Dolores's blood. Dolores rarely saw her father after her parents separated, but she knew that Juan

In the 1920s, Mexican and Filipino immigrants organized another wave of protests. These small ethnic groups achieved better wages, living, and working conditions in California, the heart of agriculture. Membership in the two unions reached twenty-five thousand each during the 1930s.

Most larger unions were led by whites. These leaders sometimes looked down on the workers they were supposed to represent, often taking bribes from growers to act against the interests of the members. Moreover, federal labor laws excluded farmworkers from rights to picket and establish unions. Eventually, the workers grew more militant as a way to protest these unfair conditions.

Growers reacted with their own violence. They hired thugs to break up union meetings with tear gas. They paid dishonest local officials to have protesters arrested. They threw union families out of labor camps and hired armed guards to kidnap, beat, and sometimes kill union organizers and members. This was the climate Dolores and César entered when they began their movement.

had become a union leader. Like his daughter, he believed that organizing workers was the only way to gain fair wages. Juan was eventually elected to the New Mexico state legislature. There he pushed for higher wages and improved working conditions for everyone. As Dolores grew older, she reconnected with her father. During that time, Juan had moved to Stockton and earned a college degree. Father and daughter took pride in each other's achievements. Dolores found inspiration in his speaking out and his commitment to furthering his education. He supported her organizing work, but he also felt that she, as a woman, was mistaken in putting career before family. Still, the two kept in touch until Juan's death.

Although the men in her life, including her father and former husbands, sometimes criticized the life she had chosen for her children, Dolores never felt that she neglected them, even though her family sometimes lived on donations of food and clothing and had little money. Dolores wanted her children to appreciate what life was like for other families and to learn to get beyond themselves and serve others.

"They became more independent. Giving kids clothes and food is one thing," she said, "but it's much more important to teach them that other people besides themselves are important. . . . So my kids know that the way that we live is poor materially speaking, but it's rich in a lot of other ways. They get to meet a lot of people and their experiences are varied."[5]

Dolores and César never accepted salaries until the union was stronger. Eventually each earned about five dollars a week. But César was right. Even the poorest farm families shared what little they could. Union families took care of each other and each other's children. "When I started working for the union I . . . knew I was going to start working without *any* money, and I wondered how I could do it. But the kids have never gone hungry."[6] With support from the farmworker community Dolores and César had launched a union. Now the real work began.

DID YOU KNOW?

César Chávez established the United Farm Workers union on a philosophy of nonviolence. He had experienced terrible poverty and racial discrimination since childhood. As an adult and parent of eight children, he wanted to change the way poor people, like his family, were treated. He read books about how leaders brought about change. He learned how Mahatma Gandhi, an Indian nationalist and spiritual leader, went on a hunger strike—refusing to eat for days at a time—in order to call attention to the cause of freedom

for his country from British control. César also followed
the example of Dr. Martin Luther King Jr., the American
activist who preached nonviolence in support of civil
rights for African Americans. King's followers were trained
never to strike back when bullied, called names, or beaten
during marches or at sit-ins in stores and restaurants—
demonstrations held to gain equal treatment for all. Like
Gandhi and King, César practiced listening as well as
talking. The soft-spoken man became the natural leader
of a new Chicano movement founded on peaceful protest.
He believed in the power of people. But as César told Fred
Ross of the CSO, "If the Movement fails, it won't be because
the growers are powerful enough to stop it, but because the
workers refuse to use their power to make it go."[7]

FIVE

TENDING THE SOIL

No More Buying Grapes!

WHEN DOLORES and César started the union, they worked without a salary for almost a year. Even when she began to take pay, Dolores earned only between five dollars and thirty-five dollars a week, not much even in the 1960s. Dolores and her family survived on money from government programs and payments from her former husbands to support the children. Food and clothing came from donations. When they had to, Dolores and César and their families earned money for their basic needs by picking cotton and grapes. Both agreed they would work just enough to get by. Their main focus was on building the union.

Laying the groundwork for a new union proved to be a slow and sometimes frustrating process. So did building union membership. To find possible members Dolores traveled wherever farmworkers gathered —pool halls, saloons, homes—any time of day or night. Many farmworkers feared being fired if their bosses found out they joined a union. Some worried that participating in a union put them and their families in danger. A few distrusted union leaders and did not believe those leaders would stick with the workers if trouble occurred. For others, even the small amount of money required for union dues was beyond their budget.

Whenever there was time, Dolores and César continued lobbying the legislature in Sacramento. After three years, Dolores noticed minor, but encouraging, improvements for farmworkers. By 1963, she had helped persuade state lawmakers to pass regulations that allowed farmworkers to receive disability and unemployment insurance. Until then, farmworkers had no right to claim these benefits, even though they were available for other citizens. If workers got sick or injured on the job, they were out of luck. If they lost a job for any reason, no matter how unfair, they lost their income. With these new regulations, the government gave farmworkers some minimal support during difficult times.

Dolores was a natural speaker on behalf of union causes, but union leaders decided to put forward César as the visible, thoughtful leader. Dolores was the hidden one: the person with the education; the one able to communicate and organize; the one with the strength to pitch César's ideas. She was also known as "La Passionaria," the passionate one, in contrast to César's calm presence.[1] Behind the scenes, Dolores was a forceful and persistent negotiator.

As membership grew, dues helped pay the members' medical bills. Richard Chávez, César's brother, worked during his spare time with other farmworkers to buy land and construct a service center. The center eventually housed a **credit union** where workers could save or borrow money. Within a few years, the union funded a retirement village for aging workers. Farmworkers later ran a radio station and published a newspaper called *El Malcriado* (in Spanish, a child who talks back to his parents).

At first, union members contented themselves with the success of two short strikes during the spring of 1965. Rose pickers in McFarland, California, wanted a pay increase and asked the union for assistance.

The union helped organize a strike of eighty-five farmworkers. After a few days, McFarland offered a wage increase but refused to recognize the union. For the time being, the farmworkers felt satisfied.

As the union—headed by Dolores and César—made gains, the growers fought back. They used their political connections to spread false claims that the union's work for justice was somehow part of a plot against the country. They spread rumors that the union advocated communism, a political system most closely associated at that time with the Soviet Union and China. Corruption in those countries had given communism a bad name. The Soviet Union, for example, had declared itself a communist nation; however, the government owned and operated everything and repressed its citizens. Since World War I, some U.S. leaders used people's fear of communism to prevent protest and stop anyone who wanted to question the government. César and Dolores were not attacking anyone's right to own a business or to earn money; they merely wanted fair treatment for farmworkers.

In 1965, members of the Filipino Agricultural Workers Organizing Committee approached César and Dolores with a problem. That September, the Coachella Valley grape growers had reduced worker pay. The growers had imported Mexican workers to pick grapes for the $1.50 an hour set by law, but they paid local workers less. Filipino farmworkers, led by Larry Itliong, refused to pick grapes for that lower rate and walked out. After ten days, the growers agreed to pay local workers the same wage as the Mexican migrants. However, the local workers received neither union recognition nor a decent contract.

By late fall, grape growers around Delano were offering the same low wage that the Coachella Valley growers had proposed before the walkout. Farmworkers from Coachella who had followed the harvest to Delano realized that the problem would keep occurring unless they signed a formal contract. On September 8, workers refused to pick grapes on nine farms. The growers brought in cheap labor to replace the strikers. Those who had left work turned to the union. Would the union support their strike against all table grape growers?

THE DELANO GRAPE STRIKE

The Filipino union and NFWA merged into one organization, the United Farm Workers of America (UFW). By joining forces, union membership broadened its reach and rose to almost six thousand farm laborers.[2]

On September 16, the union membership overwhelmingly voted to strike against table grape growers. A cry of "Viva la Huelga!" (Long Live the Strike!) rang out. The members were thrilled. This historic vote challenged those growers who believed that they could divide and control workers through fear. The grape growers, however, were not impressed. They simply hired other laborers to replace the strikers.

Within a week, several thousand union supporters had left the fields. In response, the growers drove busloads of **strikebreakers** to replace them, a tactic meant to discourage the striking workers. In some vineyards, union members managed to convince strikebreakers to leave. Growers then bribed the authorities and hired thugs to prevent strikers from approaching migrant workers to encourage them to leave the fields and join the strike. After several months, the growers offered a wage increase in an effort to stop the strike. This time, however, the farm-workers wanted more. They wanted the growers to recognize their union. And they wanted a contract.

MAJOR BREAKTHROUGH

The strike gained greater visibility once national leaders lent their support. Walter Reuther, president of the United Auto Workers union, came to Delano in the fall of 1965. In March 1966, Senator Robert F. Kennedy attended Senate hearings about migrant labor. He visited union halls, met with César, and joined marchers on **picket lines**.

In April, César organized a 340-mile march from Delano to the steps of the state capitol in Sacramento. The trek attracted public at-

Dolores and another UFW member calling out to strikebreakers
UFW Collection, 198

tention, which led to the first breakthrough: a union contract with the Schenley Wine Company in 1966. Schenley was part of a larger corporation, Schenley Industries, that made other products, many that were often given as Christmas gifts. The corporation, which already had contracts with workers in other divisions of the business, feared loss of those important holiday sales when the union called for a boycott of all Schenley products in December 1965.

Dolores organized picket lines and served as the main negotiator, becoming the first Mexican American, nonlawyer, and woman to lead negotiations for a farm labor contract. The growers who supplied Schenley with grapes eventually approved a contract that called for improved working conditions, health benefits, and an end to the use of deadly pesticides showered on crops while workers were still in the fields.

Other growers refused to follow Schenley's model of cooperation with the UFW. The DiGiorgio Corporation, for example, recognized a different union: the AFL-CIO, also known as the Teamsters. But this agreement ignored many of the issues—such as better working and living conditions—that the UFW demanded for its members. The AFL-CIO showed little concern for the problems of farmworkers. It was easier to side with growers rather than union members.

Nonviolence remained César's goal. Whenever frustrated strikers called for violence, he began a **fast**, refusing to eat as a form of protest to call attention to their cause. César hoped that his actions would show others how dedicated he was to the idea of nonviolence; he hoped to persuade others to protest peacefully. He wanted his leadership and personal appeal to spread the message of peace.

BIG-CITY SUPPORT

To make serious gains, UFW officers decided that they needed to take their struggle from the farm fields to cities across the nation. Dolores and the other union leaders believed that if American shoppers understood how badly farmworkers were treated, they would stop buying

The end of the 340-mile march from Delano to the state capitol
UFW Collection, 250. Photo: Stockton

DOLORES AND WOMEN'S RIGHTS

Dolores originally did not consider herself a voice for women. Then she met Gloria Steinem, the New York journalist who provided media attention for César during the grape strike. The two women connected a short time after Dolores arrived in New York to organize the grape boycott. "We were meeting and plotting and doing boycott lines in front of grocery stores," Gloria remembered.[3]

At the time, Gloria was also organizing like-minded women to become part of a new feminist movement. Gloria spoke out about sexist language, words that put down females. She brought awareness of the need for equal treatment of women at home and in the workplace.

Gloria helped Dolores think differently about women's rights and how they related to human rights. "When I first met her, I don't think she would have described herself as feminist," Gloria said. "But she found herself with groups that were antifeminist in addition to being anti-farmworkers. She credits me with explaining what feminism is. It was a process. But I found Dolores fierce, smart, fearless. Always with an eye on her goal. No matter what group we were with, she would have the audience chanting 'Viva La Causa.'"[4]

grapes to show support for the workers. To make this point, Dolores and other volunteers organized boycotts in several major cities.

Dolores led the grape boycott in New York City. She learned where the grapes arrived and how they were distributed. She mobilized religious, political, and peace groups to picket distribution centers and grocery stores. She arranged for picket lines of student protesters and other supporters. She approached radio and television stations and newspapers to gain more publicity. She used any means she could think of to get the public to stop buying California table grapes.

The idea of an underdog union of poor Mexican Americans led by this passionate Chicana and struggling against powerful agricultural business "captured the attention and loyalty of established labor movements in New York."[5] As the farmworkers' cause gained attention, refusing to buy table grapes from California became the just thing to do. Dolores expanded her reach—and the union's—by coordinating boycotts along the entire East Coast.

The black civil rights movement was building steam at about the same time. Average citizens learned through television and newspapers about racism and discrimination in housing, schools, voting, and jobs. Images of brutality against black citizens, especially in the South, awakened feelings against racism, bigotry, and unfairness. Concerned citizens connected the treatment of African Americans with what the farmworkers, a group primarily composed of Chicanos and Filipinos, were experiencing. People in big cities and small towns began to sympathize with individuals and groups suffering these injustices. Field-workers might be far away on farms and ranches, but they picked the fruits and vegetables that city folks ate. The national boycott started to have an impact: millions of families stopped buying table grapes.

Dolores and César spoke at universities and churches—anywhere they could get the word out about the plight of farmworkers. They held fundraisers to support the strikers and continue the boycott. Dolores's effective, rapid-fire speaking style won audiences to their side. Along the way, the union gained nationwide attention.

DIFFICULT CHOICES

Senator Robert Kennedy returned to Delano, where he met with César and Dolores, becoming a friend as well as a supporter. When Kennedy ran for president in 1968, Dolores and other union leaders helped him win the California primary election on June 4. That night Dolores accompanied Kennedy to hear his victory speech in the ballroom of the Los Angeles Ambassador Hotel. Kennedy made a point to thank Dolores and César for registering so many Chicanos to vote. But as Kennedy

A poster announcing the UFW grape boycott and a rally with César

turned to leave the hotel a murderer shot him dead. The union lost an important supporter, and Dolores lost a good friend.

Through 1968 and 1969, Dolores continued to lead the boycott. A FBI report confirmed that she was "the deciding force on the picket lines of Delano and Tulare County." Yet, at the same time, articles and books on the labor movement barely mentioned her name. Some claimed that Dolores was never mentioned because of **sexism**. While she proved herself capable within the union and in negotiations with growers, to "the unenlightened outside world she was still a woman."[6]

Sometimes her participation in union activities came at the expense of her family. Speaking engagements took her on the road nationwide. Her children lived wherever they were welcome, sometimes staying with Dolores's brother, or mother, or with union families. Her son Vincent attended a high school in New York City near her. Her daughter Lori toured with the El Teatro Campesino theater group to raise funds for strikers in California. Although sad to be separated from their mother, her children always understood the importance of her work.

Lori said, "I remember, as a child, one time talking to her about my sadness that she wasn't going to be with me on my birthday. And she said that the sacrifices we as her children make would help hundreds of other children in the future. How can you argue with something like that?" La Causa remained a family affair.[7]

Victory came on July 29, 1970, when the UFW signed a historic agreement with twenty-six major grape growers. The growers allowed farmworkers to unionize through the UFW, raised wages to $1.80 an hour, and provided other benefits. By then, the UFW counted fifty thousand dues-paying members, the largest effort ever to unionize California agriculture workers.[8] Successes by Dolores and César and their hard-working teams thrust farm labor and migrant worker rights into the national consciousness.

Farmworkers now knew that peaceful organizing and strikes could bring improved conditions—no matter how long and difficult the journey—because of the UFW's positive results with the Delano grape strike. But battles still remained against other causes, including child labor and the widespread use of pesticides. Dolores would not rest with so much left to accomplish.

DID YOU KNOW?

Music lifted the spirits of union members during tough times. When anger boiled over, many became discouraged. But one thing that instilled pride and helped unite workers was singing. Each weekly strike meeting ended with people linking hands and singing choruses of "De Colores," a traditional Spanish folk song. The song also brightened hearts on picket lines. The words celebrated all things colorful, the colors of farm life.[9] Here are selected verses:

English lyrics	Spanish lyrics
In colors, in colors	*De colores, de colores*
The fields are dressed in the spring.	*Se visten los campos en la primavera.*
In colors, in colors	*De colores, de colores*
Are the little birds that come from outside.	*Son los pajaritos que vienen de afuera.*
In colors, in colors	*De colores, de colores*
Is the rainbow that we see shining.	*Es el arco iris que vemos lucir.*
In colors, in colors	*De colores, de colores*
Yes, black and white and red and blue and brown.	*Sí, de blanco y negro y rojo y azul y castano.*
All the colors, colors	*Son colores, son colores*
From people laughing, and shaking hands.	*De gente que rie, ye estrecha la mano.*
All the colors, colors	*Son colores, son colores*
From the people who know freedom.	*De gente que sabe de la libertad.*

SIX

THINNING THE SHOOTS

The Fight Continues

T HE EARLY 1970S saw some of the bitterest struggles for union recognition. Growers continued to hire thugs to keep union representatives from talking to workers in the fields. They threatened workers
and union leaders alike. Sometimes thugs visited workers' homes and
communities to frighten them with threats of violence.

Growers also used their wealth to spread antiunion messages. Money
that could have been spent on fair salaries and better living conditions
for workers instead went to bribes for local politicians and law enforce-
ment. Companies such as Gallo wine chose to spend thousands of dollars on full-page newspaper ads, urging customers to stop supporting
the boycott. César shot back with words of his own: "Their millions
will not buy them the truth."[1]

Gallo, like other grape and lettuce growers, bussed in strikebreakers
who knew little of the dangers they faced. Two farmworkers died in 1973
—electrocuted on untested machinery. Dolores claimed that a union
contract would have prevented companies from ordering people to use
such unsafe equipment. She spread word of other accidents, including

44

Dolores visiting a picket line
UFW Collection, 189. Photo: *El Macriado* staff

some that caused additional worker deaths. Her message about safety began to take hold within the nonfarm community.

As the UFW aroused sympathy and gained more members, Teamster union interest in representing farmworkers grew. This was the same national union that previously had negotiated special, secret deals with growers and had accepted contracts that only pretended to benefit workers. Teamster deals may have raised worker pay, but they undercut worker rights and left inhumane job conditions in place. Farmworkers still had little say in how they were treated.[2]

Dolores preferred to educate others and develop new leaders for the union, but César needed her political and negotiating skills elsewhere.

THE CULTURE OF LA CAUSA

AS THE Delano grape strike and lettuce boycott came to a close, something surprising occurred. Awareness spread about the situation of farmworkers, and their movement for justice, arts, and culture developed around La Causa. Supporters wrote songs, chants, theater productions, and stories about labor heroes, especially César and Dolores.[3] They also created dances, which Dolores loved. These artistic expressions reminded supporters that "regardless what happens, we can always go on strike and don't forget it."[4]

Supporters among gringos wrote songs, too. Woody Guthrie, Pete Seeger, and feminist and folk singer Kristin Lems created songs that highlighted the importance of farm labor. Lems concentrated on women—on their contributions on the farm and as forces for change. In one song, "Farmer," she touched on another injustice, one that took away farms owned by a man and a woman together, if the man died. Consider the last two stanzas:

> I know we women, we ain't been in the know
> But we're no fools as far as farmin goes
> The crop don't know no woman's work or man's
> There ain't no law can take me from my land

> Cause I'm a farmer, I been one all my life
> Call me a farmer, and not a farmer's wife
> The plough and hoe left their patterns on my hand
> No one can tell me this is not my land
> This is my land!

The historic gains that farmworkers had made during the early 1970s were under assault on several fronts. Dolores spent considerable time in Sacramento and Washington, D.C., fending off numerous court cases initiated by growers and larger unions. Armed with expensive lawyers, these groups threatened to erase the progress the UFW had made.

SÍ SE PUEDE!

In California, Dolores and the union helped Jerry Brown win the 1974 governorship. In turn, Brown pushed the state legislature to pass the 1975 California Agricultural Labor Relations Act. The law granted California farmworkers the right to hold union elections to decide which union the members preferred to represent them. Before that, the Teamsters had bullied workers into voting for their representation. The following summer, a majority of farmworkers voted to reject the Teamsters.[5] California's historic act became the first law to recognize the right of agricultural employees to negotiate with a group of employers to agree on salaries and work conditions. Even with the act, though, employers continued to try to block unions from exercising these rights.

Dolores traveled to Washington, D.C., to seek support in Congress from both Democrats and Republicans. Whenever she heard about a state law to limit farmworker unions, she'd rush to that state. In 1972, when the Arizona legislature passed a bill to stop farmworkers from striking and holding boycotts during harvest seasons, Dolores traveled to Phoenix, the state capital.

Dolores asked to meet with Governor John Williams before a union protest rally that was scheduled for noon that day. She hoped that she and César could persuade Williams to refuse to sign the bill into law. "Well, the governor signed the bill at nine o'clock in the morning without even meeting with us," Dolores said. "Now we're getting everybody registered to vote. We're going to recall the governor and turn the state upside-down. . . . Every time they try to do something against the union it works in our favor."[6]

César responded by staying in Arizona and beginning a fast. Dolores remained by his side as he grew weaker each day. Every night, supporters filled the Santa Rita Center in Phoenix for a mass. Famous civil rights leaders, including Senator Eugene McCarthy and Coretta Scott King, came to pay tribute and show support. After twenty-four days, César's doctor ordered him to end the fast and go into the hospital. His heartbeat was irregular. His kidneys showed signs of failing. The fast forever weakened the union leader. Yet, even during his suffering, César issued a statement that his fast served as an example of farmworker suffering.

The fast proved a peaceful way to mobilize labor and religious leaders. Because of public attention it attracted to the workers' cause, the farmworkers gathered enough signatures to force an election to recall, or force out, the governor. But the wealthy growers and the state **attorney general** got in the way. The attorney general, Richard Kleindienst, ordered that both Governor Williams and the law remain in place.

The UFW leaders felt that the situation was hopeless. "No se puede," or, "We can't," someone said. Dolores had her own response. "Sí, sí se puede," or "Yes, yes we can," she repeated. The phrase stuck and became a slogan and rallying cry for farmworkers from then on.[7]

BABY STEPS OF PROGRESS

Within a few years, Dolores and the UFW saw benefits from their new contracts. "We set up the hiring hall," Dolores said. "We were able to plan the workforce, so the farmer doesn't hire say six hundred people to do a job in two weeks when they can hire three hundred to do the job in two-and-a-half months. So you expand the length of the workforce. Some miraculous things happened in Delano after we got those contracts. Farmers bought their homes in the area where they worked. Kids went to school. We had eleven children of farmworkers go to college after the first year that we got the contract. Migrancy is forced migrancy. People don't like to drag their kids around the country. But they have no job security when they can get fired and have to keep moving."[8]

Richard Chávez pointing to the hard-earned union label on the box of grapes
UFW Collection, 26490.

Along the way, Dolores began a romantic relationship with Richard Chávez, César's brother. Dolores had finally found a true partner and a lasting relationship. She gave birth to four more children with Richard: Juanita, Maria Elena, Ricky, and Camila. In addition to becoming a Chicana folk hero, she was a role model for working mothers everywhere. Dolores and Richard stayed together until Richard's death in 2011.

AN IMPERFECT LEADER

Dolores gained a reputation as a tough negotiator. But she also could be unpredictable and disorganized. She'd lose everything from wallets and clothing to important papers. Her daughter Lori liked to call her "the disorganized organizer."[9]

If Dolores needed to emphasize a point during contract meetings, she called surprise demonstrations. Farmworkers marched in with banners, chanting union slogans and songs. Her emotions often rose to the surface. Sometimes, she shouted and cried. She insulted. She refused to compromise. But she got results. "Dolores Huerta is physically and mentally fearless," César said.[10]

Some tactics angered growers, but other people found her passion inspiring. One representative of the grape growers insisted in a sexist rant that the devil possessed Dolores. "Dolores Huerta is crazy," he raged. "She's a violent woman, where women, especially Mexican women, are usually peaceful and pleasant. You can't live wrought up like she does and not be crazy." California legislator John Vasconellos found her "too quick to attack, too reluctant to listen." But another member of the California legislature, Nicholas Petris, said, "Huerta is a brave woman. She's a believer, not a broker, for her cause."[11]

Dolores's children often said that she was their hero. In addition to developing independence, they learned how to care for others and work in the community. Her children knew how to be feminists, because their mother lived that role. "What I love about my hero is that she doesn't try to be perfect," said her daughter Juanita. "She will be the first to admit her faults."[12]

Dolores herself understood that she could be trouble. She told one reporter, "My personal life is a mess."[13] On another occasion, she admitted, "I know I have a terrible temper." Even her way of encouraging others sometimes sounded angry. "Don't be a marshmallow," she would yell at marches and on picket lines. "Walk the street with us into history. Stop being vegetables. Work for justice. Viva the boycott!"[14]

Sometimes the personality and skills that succeeded during contract meetings on picket lines clashed with César's calmer methods. The two had a complicated relationship. On the one hand, they shared a vision and a passion. They both believed in nonviolence and justice. But they often differed and sometimes argued on how to achieve these goals.

"César fired me fifteen times, and I must have quit about ten." Dolores said. "Then, we'll call each other up and get back to work. There have been times when I should have fought harder. When he tells me now, 'you're getting impossible, arguing all the time,' I say, 'you haven't seen anything yet.' . . . Because from now on I'm going to fight really, really hard when I believe something. I can be wrong, too, but at least it will be on the record how I felt."[15]

DID YOU KNOW?

Cinco de Mayo, or the fifth of May, is a holiday observed more by Mexican Americans than in Mexico itself. It celebrates the day in 1862 when the Mexican army defeated a French force during the Franco-Mexican War. Mexican peasants—men and women armed only with *machetes*—fought off well-armed soldiers. Dolores believes that Mexican Americans relate to the holiday because it is an example of a victory over injustice. "These were basically campesinos, farmworkers, and I think that that's why it's significant, . . . because of the oppression of Mexican Americans . . . . As long as that message can get out that poor people can take power, can control their destinies, I think that's an important message."[16]

SEVEN

WEEDING THE FIELDS

Danger Ahead

N ATIONWIDE RECOGNITION proved helpful to the UFW, especially by making César a household name. Dolores remained in
the background, at least as far as the public outside California was concerned. Locally, she continued to rack up successes. She negotiated
contracts. She organized marches and boycotts. These successes, small
and large, inspired her to push harder. She knew there were many
wrongs yet to right.

Farmers and ranchers that recognized unions required constant
supervision to ensure that they actually followed the contract agree-
ments. Most growers used every means possible to weaken the union.
One such effort took advantage of a **loophole** in the National Labor
Relations Act (NLRA), a law passed in 1935 with the intention of protecting unions. The law set national guidelines for organizing unions
and bargaining between union representatives and employers. In addition, it created an independent National Labor Relations Board to
oversee these rules. But before final passage of the law, powerful growers persuaded Congress to remove farmworkers from the bill. This lack

of farmworker protection allowed lawyers hired by the growers to stop union advances in court. Court cases cost the UFW dearly in money and time. Blocked in the courts, the union and its committed members found other ways to defend farmworkers against abuse.

Dolores encountered another problem that complicated contracts. New more efficient machines now performed jobs once handled by farmworkers. In the 1960s, farmworkers accounted for 41 percent of the agricultural workforce. Forty-five thousand workers harvested 2.2 million tons of tomatoes. Into the twenty-first century, farmworkers made up only 2 percent of the agricultural workforce. By 2000, California growers hired only five thousand pickers to harvest a tomato crop of twelve million tons.[1] Still, Dolores never lost faith.

FARMWORKERS AND THE ENVIRONMENT

Dolores was one of the earliest voices to sound the alarm about poisons in the food supply. One source was pesticides, chemicals sprayed on crops to boost their growth and kill invading insects and diseases. Often, farm owners scheduled spraying while farmworkers hoed, thinned, and picked in the fields. Workers were told these weed killers were "medicine" for plants and would never hurt humans.[2]

Dolores knew differently. Spraying crops with pesticides posed dangers for farmworkers. Pesticides also threatened the health of consumers and the environment. Dolores's research discovered that eight hundred thousand people died each year from direct or indirect effects of pesticides. Many more, like weeders and pickers, suffered ill effects from exposure to the chemicals. Workers displayed high rates of skin diseases, certain cancers, and birth defects in their children.

But local doctors associated with growers never reported these conditions. They documented other causes for worker illnesses. "What we have is large agribusinesses . . . who are making money from agriculture, and they really want to control the food supply," Dolores told journalist Studs Terkel.[3] That need for control put the lives of workers at risk.

Pesticide spraying in farm fields
UFW Collection, 253. Photo: *El Macriado* staff

Another problem with food safety came from poor sanitation. Dolores worried about the entire food chain, from farms to stores. Farmworkers' hands picked and packed crops in the field. They loaded the crates of foods onto boxcars bound for markets. Dolores explained. "Now if that food has been picked where there isn't a toilet, that food may be contaminated. That's why it's so important to get those contracts, so that the farmers can have their toilets and washing facilities. We [the UFW] send our medical teams . . . to the labor camps and give people tests for tuberculosis. If there were any [signs] of disease, we pulled [workers] out of the labor force. This is because we care."[4]

THEATER OF HUELGA

The concept of *huelga,* or labor strike, was an important part of Chicano union culture. Dolores and other protesters waved signs reading, "Viva la Huelga!" Chicano union meetings opened and closed with the chant in a show of solidarity—with the movement, with strikers, with each other.

Nobody spread the feeling of huelga like the theater group El Teatro Campesino, whose actors got their start on UFW picket lines. El Teatro Campesino performed its first short skits on flatbed trucks in front of picket lines and in union halls during the 1965 Delano grape strike. The group toured throughout the California farm region, raising funds to "dramatize the plight and cause of the farmworkers," earning the 1969 Obie Award for portraying "the politics of survival."[5]

El Teatro Campesino, under the leadership of Luis Valdez, became an instant hit with a wide audience, earning national, and then international, attention over the next few decades. Small productions expanded into musicals incorporating corridos, dances, and plays. Artists performed on stage, on television, and in movies, sometimes with other groups from as far away as France and England. More recently, the company has made multimedia and digital productions for multicultural audiences. But its emphasis still remains on social change through the arts, a concept that began with huelga.

LIFE-ALTERING MARCH

Throughout the 1980s, Dolores filled her calendar with travel, speaking engagements, fund-raising, and lobbying politicians in California and throughout the nation. She cofounded Radio Campesina, the UFW radio station.[6] After meeting Gloria Steinem in the 1970s, Dolores added gender equality to the long list of causes she championed.

In 1985, Dolores worked for passage of the Immigration Reform Act. Until then, hundreds of thousands of immigrant farmworkers had paid U.S. taxes, yet they obtained none of the benefits usually accorded to tax-paying citizens. "Why is it that farmworkers feed the nation but they can't get food stamps?" she would ask crowds.[7] The new act helped balance this unfair situation.

Small successes often came at great physical costs. Dolores was arrested twenty-two times. Thugs hired to stop protests threatened and often shoved and assaulted her. During marches, wealthy growers occasionally gave secret payments to corrupt police officers who—unlike the honest officers who obeyed their duty to protect citizens—treated Dolores and other protesters violently.

The worst attack occurred in 1988. Dolores led a march in San Francisco to protest against presidential candidate George H. W. Bush, in part because of his policies regarding pesticides. Bush claimed to be a friend of Chicanos, yet he opposed the union and farmworkers who wanted protections from pesticide exposure.

The candidate's staff, of course, wanted to prevent the protest. Although the march was peaceful, something triggered security officers to push into the orderly crowd. Dolores got caught in the rush and was beaten to the ground. An emergency vehicle whisked her into emergency surgery, where doctors worked to save her life. Dolores suffered several broken ribs and a ruptured **spleen**. She lost so much blood that she could have died. But she didn't.

Her recovery was a long, slow process. Dolores drew strength from her fighting spirit. And, in her usual way, she turned a terrible situation

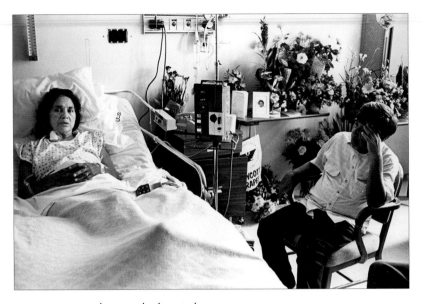

César visiting Dolores in the hospital
UFW Collection, 191. Photo: Victor Aleman

into an opportunity to push for justice. By chance, a local television station crew had filmed her beating. This record of the beating gave Dolores proof enough to sue the city and receive an award settlement of $825,000. But Dolores had not sued for the money. She wanted to make sure that no one else attending a peaceful protest would be abused that way. Publicity from the video and the court case helped her succeed in requiring better training and discipline for police.[8]

After the election, public interest in farmworker causes and unions in general lessened; their stories faded from the news. But the actions of the UFW during the election had introduced the concept of worker rights to larger segments of the population, and the union's successes further emboldened the Mexican American community. As Dolores's energy returned, she resumed her work with the UFW.

DID YOU KNOW?

Over many years, groups like the UFW have used different peaceful tactics to encourage individuals to further their causes. Some march, while others hold sit-ins, walk away from work, or lock doors to their places of employment to keep owners and replacement workers out. Today, many groups protest online or write letters to newspapers, magazines, and television stations. Others ask citizens to sign petitions—both online and on street corners—to support their causes. These petitions are then sent to state or national legislators to tell those legislators how their voters want them to act. In similar acts of peaceful protest, students have walked out of class, signed petitions addressed to the school administration, written letters to local newspapers, and raised their arms or kneeled at sports games to show support for a cause.

EIGHT

SPREADING MORE SEEDS

Expanding the Cause

B ETWEEN 1991 AND 1993, Dolores took a break from UFW activities and focused her attention on women's rights. In 1987, Eleanor Smeal and others involved with *Ms.* magazine had joined with the women's group Feminist Majority to form a foundation devoted to advancing legal, social, and political equality between genders to empower women and girls. Dolores was a founding member.

The Feminist Majority Foundation (FMF) conducted research into every aspect of women's roles. Armed with poll results, foundation members turned that research into action plans in numerous categories, including public policy, reproductive health, and prevention of violence against females.[1] Those plans became the Feminist Majority's Feminization of Power program.

One telling result of their research showed that, of the 325 federal judges whom President Ronald Reagan had appointed in 1987, 278 were white men, 29 were white females, five were African American, and none were Hispanic. These figures pointed to the terrible lack of diversity in a key branch of government that affects the lives of everyone in the country.[2] Dolores targeted the lack of Hispanic representation. She began traveling the country, encouraging Hispanic women to enter politics and urging Hispanic voters to support them.

Dolores's involvement with FMF grew out of her earlier connection with Gloria Steinem and her belief in equality for everyone. Before meeting Gloria, Dolores had assumed women belonged anywhere they chose. "Excluding women, protecting them, keeping women at home, that's the middle-class way. Poor people's movements have always had whole families on the line, ready to move at a moment's notice, with more courage because that's all we had," Dolores said. "It's a class—not an ethnic—thing."[3]

Before joining the FMF, Dolores had questioned whether saying that she was a feminist would mean she was against women having children rather than pursuing careers. "I still believe you are supposed to conceive children," she said. "Poor people think big families are strong families, and I love my kids."[4] Once Dolores understood that most feminists supported a woman's decision to have children or not to have children, she was on board. She believed it was a personal issue.

A COLLEAGUE AND HERO DIES

On April 23, 1993, César died in his sleep. By then, he and Dolores had spent more than thirty years working together. She and thirty-five thousand family, friends, and supporters walked for three miles behind his casket. Dolores spoke to the crowd about how proud she was of him and the union they had founded together. César's loss hit his family, the farm community, and Dolores, in particular, very hard.

Many feared the end of the UFW without César. Dolores knew better. In a strange twist, César's death created renewed interest in his life and his beliefs, beliefs that he shared with Dolores. "César believed . . . that you can't really feel the pain of the poor unless you are one of them," Dolores said.[5] She felt the same way. But Dolores was her own person, and she followed the ideal to "be herself" that had begun with

A quiet moment for César with his dogs, Huelga and Boycott
UFW Collection, 216. Photo: Cathy Murphy

her mother's words years earlier.[6] Dolores's belief in personal freedom was linked to her beliefs in the importance of strong community ties and the power of many working together, whatever the cause.

This commitment to self and community led Dolores to back the next UFW president, Arturo Rodriguez, César's son-in-law. Before César died, Arturo had pushed the UFW leadership to strengthen the union with more forceful campaigns, like those the union had engaged in when it was first formed. Once again, Dolores became actively involved in the union (in truth, she had never left), helping to recruit new members and build grassroots support on more farms.

Two of Dolores's passions, farmworker treatment and women's rights, came together when the UFW joined a discrimination lawsuit aimed at berry farms in Salinas County, California. The women behind the lawsuit claimed that foremen preferred men when hiring. Once hired, women earned less because foremen gave them fewer hours. Women were also banned from farm jobs, such as truck or tractor driver, irrigator, or stacker, that paid more. During the campaign, Dolores held marathon meetings, led marches, and advised young organizers who faced threats from growers when they entered the fields to talk with pickers.[7]

In 1995, VCNM Farms in Salinas elected to plow under one-quarter of its crops and lay off workers rather than submit to the union vote. The UFW changed tactics. Instead of going after individual growers, the union chose to organize at large shipping companies that packaged and distributed all the berries. Dolores, Arturo, and César's brother Richard led supporters into Watsonville shouting, "Long live the strawberry pickers!"[8] At about the same time, UFW leaders traveled throughout California, Florida, and Alabama on behalf of mushroom pickers and to continue the seventeen-year-old battle with lettuce growers. La Causa was spreading again.

These new efforts produced hard-earned results. By the close of 1997, the UFW had added five thousand new members and successfully signed fifteen new contracts, which Dolores happily negotiated. Meanwhile, she continued in her roles as lobbyist, strike organizer, fund raiser, union executive, and speaker.

As Arturo later told a reporter, "Early in 1970, César Chávez said [Dolores] is totally fearless, both physically and mentally. A quarter of a century later she shows no sign of slowing down. [Dolores] is an enduring symbol of the farmworker movement."[9]

DOLORES STEPS DOWN FROM THE UFW

Dolores stayed with the union until 1999. That year, she gave up her formal UFW duties. The UFW renamed her "vice-president **emeritus**," granting her a position of honor that freed her from daily responsibilities. This allowed her to devote more time to work on behalf of her other causes, including campaigns to elect public officials who supported

Dolores Huerta speaking at a march

UFW Collection, 200

those causes. That included Chicanas, women in general, and men such as Al Gore, who was running for president of the United States.

Dolores refused to slow down. Often sleeping only four hours a night, she traveled anywhere, anytime, to promote the cause of civil rights. "She's **indefatigable**," said Eleanor Smeal, president of the Feminist Majority Foundation. "I don't know of any other leader who has the schedule she has. . . . She'll fly in from South America on the redeye for a board meeting, . . . If you say, 'Can you stay another day?' she will. Huerta spends most of her downtime up in the air, reading newspapers and a book or two as she flies to her next destination."[10]

DEADLY SCARE

Dolores rarely pampered herself when she got sick. But in October 2000, her body suffered a devastating blow. A blood clot formed and traveled from her heart to her abdomen, bursting a blood vessel. Doctors cleared the clot, but the injury left her unable to do much on her own. "I had to learn how to walk, talk, and how to eat," she said.[11] Nothing stopped Dolores for long, however. From her hospital bed, she called on followers to vote for Gore.

Recovery took longer than expected. But after a year of therapy, Dolores regained all her abilities—especially talking. She resumed a reduced but still active schedule. Dolores was now into her seventies. Still she crisscrossed the nation arguing against government policies that harmed women, immigrants, the poor, and farmworkers.

In 2002, Dolores led a 165-mile (266 km) march to Sacramento through a relentless sun and temperatures that rose to 100 degrees F (37 degrees C). Her presence, she felt, was necessary to pressure Governor Gray Davis to sign landmark state legislation that would provide farmworkers with greater ability to bargain. He did, but only after Dolores and hundreds of workers kept up a sit-in for several weeks on the capitol steps. Governor Davis and other government officials took notice of Dolores and her untiring commitment to education and better living conditions for working families—the same things she had wanted for her first students. The following year, Governor Davis appointed Dolores to the University of California Board of Regents.

THE DOLORES HUERTA FOUNDATION

In 2002, Dolores was awarded the Puffin/Nation Prize for Creative Citizenship from The Puffin Foundation and The Nation Institute for her lifetime of service. (Dolores being Dolores, the nominating committee had difficulty reaching her to tell her about the prize. She was on the road again.) The award included a gift of $100,000. Rather than personally keeping all the money, Dolores launched the Dolores Huerta Foundation (DHF), with her youngest daughter, Camila Chávez, as president.

The foundation offered educational and training programs designed to strengthen communities facing different types of hardship. Further, the foundation became a way for Dolores to control her own message—about her personal life and about her goals and passions. Since its founding, DHF has increased Dolores's voice, extending her influence.

With her usual determination, Dolores presented the foundation's vision at a gathering of California politicians and activists in labor and immigration rights. The new organization sought to train activists at the grassroots level to work for just causes. "More than ever, we need to develop grass roots, **indigenous** leaders," Dolores said. "People need to know they have power, and it needs to come from the bottom up."[12] The crowd responded with applause, songs, and thumping beats.

The foundation's main office opened in downtown Bakersfield, California. Workers established models for action in rural communities. They enlisted public officials to bring more benefits to their communities. All the while, organizers engaged those who lived in these communities to act on their own behalf, much as the UFW had done.

DOLORES AND THE MOVIES

OVER THE YEARS, Dolores incorporated whatever means worked best to promote her messages of social justice. She was interviewed on television shows and participated in about ten documentary movies and videos. The first was made in 1997 (*The Fight in the Fields*); a later film focused on César's advocacy of farmworker rights (*Song for César*, 2017). More recently Dolores spoke out about women in a television miniseries (*Makers: Women Who Make America*, 2013) and about Latino causes; both were covered in a June 25, 2013, *Frontline* television interview about women and farm foremen.

Education also has been a long-running priority for Dolores. In 2008, she consulted with the Southern Poverty Law Center's Teaching Tolerance education program. The result was a documentary film and teaching kit, *Viva La Causa*. The film dealt with the UFW's nonviolent grape strike and boycott and the union's march for human rights, providing messages of empowerment to young viewers. Rosario Dawson, a Latina actress who had worked with Dolores promoting Latino voters with Vote/Latino, played Dolores in the 2014 movie *César Chávez*; America Ferrera played César's wife, Helen. Since the movie, Rosario began pushing for a separate movie about Dolores. In 2017, the movie *Dolores* portrayed its subject as a social justice pioneer.

In the years that followed, the foundation refocused activities around four main areas that limited justice for many individuals. Sexism and unequal pay still dogged the nation. Immigration rights were tearing communities apart. The **LGBT** (lesbian, gay, bisexual, transgender) community proclaimed their right to live without fear and to love whom they choose. And many poor communities still lacked access to schools that provided the quality of education that could promise their children a better future.

MORE UFW STRUGGLES

Dolores supported union efforts whenever she could. Battles continued, as huge corporations that now owned much of the farmland refused to recognize unions or collective bargaining. The UFW still struggled to attain higher pay, overtime wages, and days off for workers during a harvest week of backbreaking work.

Between 2005 and 2013, eighty farmworkers died from heat-related causes. Although California health laws required easy access to water sources, shade for workers when temperatures climbed above eighty degrees, and regular breaks when temperatures reached more than ninety-five degrees, many growers thought they could fulfill these regulations by putting shade and water within a mile or two of where picking occurred. However, because a worker's pay often was based on how much they picked, many could not afford to stop work and travel to the shade and water, even for their own safety.

SAD TIMES

On July 27, 2011, Dolores suffered a terrible loss. Her longtime partner and father of her four youngest children, Richard Chávez, died. Richard had worked alongside Dolores, ever since he designed the United Farm Workers' well-known Aztec eagle logo decades earlier. He had been a tireless activist—with Dolores and on his own.

Dolores lost her soulmate and dancing partner, but she never lost her commitment to La Causa. Her new chapter began.

DID YOU KNOW?

Visitors to California can see a nine-foot-tall statue of César Chávez and Dolores Huerta on Main Street in downtown Napa overlooking the Napa River. The massive bronze statue shines in the sun as a testament to these two key farmworker leaders. Local sculptor Mario Chiodo created the larger-than-life figures. Napa developer Michael Holcomb commissioned the statue to spotlight Latino worker contributions and the two people who worked so hard to improve the workers' lives.

NINE

ANOTHER HARVEST

More Mountains to Climb

Losing Richard was a blow. But Dolores refuses to slow down, participating in marches and lobbying as hard as she had when she was a young teacher. Dolores continues to prove that age is meaningless, just a number. Well into her eighties, she dances the Macarena and sings *De Colores*. Equally important, she still ruffles feathers.

Younger Spanish-speaking leaders sometimes question her choices, especially in politics. But whatever their disagreements, they recognize that now they have choices—and a national voice. Today, Latinos and Latinas fill leading political and corporate roles. They see themselves on television and in pop culture. They march for their causes because women, immigrants, and Spanish-speaking citizens like Dolores paved the way.

Few of these options were available when Dolores first started battling existing norms. Even voices that never agreed with her gained visibility because she—and other women like her—spoke out. Dolores provided a role model for self-esteem, by being herself. She offered direction to strong girls and women. She proclaimed that females, including Latinas, had choices—in matters of education, professions, gender, and family.

Whenever Dolores decides to put up her feet to rest (which rarely happens), her foundation continues her ongoing fight against injustice. Dolores's daughter Camila and son Emilio participate in the varied activities the foundation promotes, including programs for gender equality, fair wages, a healthy environment, improved education, and financial literacy, as well as political empowerment. Dolores considers these causes essential foundations for a healthy, prosperous life for every race, religion, and gender.

Her eleven children are now adults. They thrive in a variety of professions: doctor, lawyer, massage therapist, foundation leader, teacher, public health specialist, filmmaker, musician, and poet. They all believe that their mother had instilled in them a "sense of civic duty" and a belief in doing their best, no matter what their chosen field. Their mother might have missed birthdays and holidays when they were growing up, but they feel that by her being a committed role model she inspired them to believe in themselves. From her they learned that anything is possible if someone works hard enough for it. Now Dolores is a role model to two more generations: her fifteen grandchildren and four great-grandchildren.[1]

But speaking her mind and being a civil rights activist wasn't always easy. As one reporter noted about Dolores, "Living as an activist has meant defying her family and redefining her role as a mother. It has meant poverty. It has been a life etched by threats, protest marches, police brutality, and imprisonment. But it has also brought triumphs—hers and the people she continues to serve."[2]

Dolores's simple words and strong belief in justice have carried on. She counts improvements in farmworker wages, clean drinking water, toilets in the fields, decent housing, health benefits, environmental policies, and freedom to work without sexual harassment among her credits. She boasts that 2015 was a banner year for elected Latino members of the U.S. Congress. That year, voters elected twenty-nine Hispanic candidates to the U.S. House of Representatives and three more to the Senate. Latinos represented 17 percent of the entire U.S. population and occupied 8 percent of the seats in Congress.[3] Latinas filled elected offices in state and local governments, and President Obama appointed Justice Sonia Sotomayor to the Supreme Court. Dolores does not take credit for all these accomplishments. But throughout her life she pushed for inclusion of more Latinos and women in government. She showed what a strong woman can do. When she first began, there were few or no Latina role models. Now there are.

Years ago and many marches earlier, Dolores Huerta summed up her life best: "I would like to be viewed as a woman who cares for fellow humans," she told one reporter. "We must use our lives to make the world a better place, not just to acquire things. That is what we are put on earth for."[4] And that has been how she lived her life. Viva La Causa!

DID YOU KNOW?

In the 1930s and '40s there was a famous dance team made up of Ginger Rogers and Fred Astaire. Back then, there was little equality between the sexes. Men received full credit for accomplishments, even those that should have been shared equally with women. Over time, some people joked that Ginger did everything that Fred did—but she danced backwards and in three-inch heels. Today many have noticed a similarity between the team of Fred and Ginger and that of Dolores Huerta and César Chávez. Dolores did everything César did—but she did it while raising eleven children.

FINALLY, RECOGNITION

DOLORES HUERTA finally received the recognition she deserves. Curiously, honors flowed freer in the years after César's death. Once his voice was gone, the range of jobs and decisions shepherded by Dolores became apparent. Sexism had kept her hidden.

Dolores continues to receive honors for vigorously seeking justice. But she still believes working for the good of others is much more important than all the money and honors anyone can acquire. To honor that spirit, four elementary schools in California and Fort Worth, Texas, and one high school in Pueblo, Colorado, were named after her. Nine universities gave her honorary doctorates. Her other honors include the following:

1984 California State Senate Outstanding Labor Leader Award

1993 National Women's Hall of Fame Inductee
American Civil Liberties Union Roger Baldwin Medal of Liberty Award
Eugene V. Debs Foundation Outstanding American Award
Ellis Island Medal of Freedom Award

1997 *Ms.* magazine Woman of the Year (one of three honorees)

1998 Eleanor D. Roosevelt Award for Human Rights
The 100 Most Important Women of the TwentiethCentury from the *Ladies Home Journal*

2002 The Puffin Foundation Ltd. and The Nation Institute Puffin/ Nation Prize for Creative Citizenship

2003 University of California Board of Regents Appointee

2012 Presidential Medal of Freedom

2013 California Hall of Fame Inductee

2015 *One Life: Dolores Huerta,* the eleventh exhibit in the National Portrait Gallery's series and the first devoted to a Latina

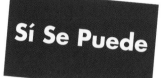

Sí Se Puede

Dolores's Timeline

1930	Dolores is born on April 10 in Dawson, New Mexico.
1935	Dolores's mother and father divorce. Her mother moves Dolores and her brothers to Stockton, California.
1945	Dolores experiences racial prejudice in high school, altering her view of the world.
1949	Dolores begins classes at Stockton College, later known as San Joaquin Delta Community College.
1950	Dolores marries her high school boyfriend, Ralph Head, just before her twentieth birthday. She and Ralph have two daughters, Celeste and Lori, but divorce within a few years.
1955	Dolores meets Frank Ross and launches the Stockton chapter of the Community Service Organization (CSO), a group dedicated to fighting for economic improvement for Chicanos. She quits teaching.
1956	Dolores meets Ventura Huerta through the CSO. The couple marry and have five children: Fidel, Emilio, Vincent, Alicia, and Angela. This marriage ends after several years.
1960	Dolores works with César Chávez, helping to organize the 1960 voter registration drive in California, during which 150,000 voters are registered. She develops skills in making speeches, lobbying government officials, and organizing.
1962	Dolores cofounds the National Farm Workers Association, later renamed United Agricultural Workers (UFW) Organizing Committee, with César Chávez.
1964	The Bracero Program, which began in 1942 as the Mexican Farm Labor Program, ends.
1965	The UFW holds its first two successful strikes, but McFarland rose pickers refuse to recognize the union. Dolores directs the

UFW national boycott connected with the Delano grape strike, becoming the lead spokesperson and promoter informing consumers about the plight of farmworkers. The UFW merges with the Filipino union led by Larry Itliong for the strike.

1966   César and Dolores organize a 340-mile march from Delano to the steps of the state capitol in Sacramento. Dolores negotiates the first union contract with the Schenley Wine Company.

1968–1969   Dolores mobilizes the grape boycott promotion, resulting in her directing the entire East Coast boycott operations.

1970   The United Farm Workers sign a historic agreement with twenty-six table grape growers.

1972   Dolores co-chairs the California delegation to the Democratic National Convention held to decide the party's candidate for U.S. president. This places her in a key position to effect political power for Latinos.

1973   Dolores attacks abusive practices of growers, including the use of child labor and lack of worker safety. She and Richard Chávez begin their longtime romantic relationship that produces four children: Juanita, Maria Elena, Ricky, and Camila.

1974   Dolores and UFW members help to elect Jerry Brown as California governor.

1975   Union members help Governor Brown pass the California Agricultural Labor Relations Act, the first state law to grant farmworkers the right of collective bargaining.

1988   Dolores receives a life-threatening beating at a rally in San Francisco protesting presidential candidate George H. W. Bush's ideas about unions and farmworkers. She sues the city and wins a cash settlement and promises of better crowd-control training for the police force.

1993   Dolores is inducted into the National Women's Hall of Fame, the first Latina to be so honored.

1998   *Ms.* magazine names Dolores one of three "Women of the Year."

Ladies Home Journal chooses Dolores as one of the "100 Most Important Women of the Twentieth Century."

President Bill Clinton chooses Dolores as one of five recipients of the Eleanor Roosevelt Award for Human Rights.

2002	Dolores receives the second annual Puffin/Nation Prize for Creative Citizenship. The prize's $100,000 award allows her to establish the Dolores Huerta Foundation.
2011	Richard Chávez, Dolores's longtime partner and father of their four children—Camila, Juana, Maria Elena, and Ricky—dies on July 27.
2012	Dolores appears in the documentary *Brothers on the Line*, which tells the story of three brothers—Walter, Roy, and Victor Reuther—and their work for social justice.
	President Barack Obama honors Dolores with the Presidential Medal of Freedom on May 29.
2015	The National Portrait Gallery, Washington, D.C., opens a ten-month exhibit titled *One Life: Dolores Huerta* to coincide with the fiftieth anniversary of the 1965 grape strike. This is the eleventh installment in the gallery's series and the first devoted to a Latina.
2016	Dolores attends the 2016 Democratic National Convention as a guest speaker in support of candidate Hillary Clinton for president.
	Dolores participates in the making of the documentary *Song for César, the Movement and the Music* about the role music, musicians, artists, and other supporters played in assisting César Chávez and the growth of the United Farm Workers union.

Glossary

barrio: neighborhood with many Spanish-speaking residents

boycott: an organized group protest to refuse to buy or handle goods or co-operate with or participate in a policy or event. In Dolores's case, this involved discouraging people from buying table grapes from California growers.

Bracero Program: *Bracero* is Spanish for manual worker. In 1942, the U.S. and Mexican governments affirmed a labor agreement that allowed temporary worker status to Mexican farmworkers so they could pick crops in the United States. This agreement, formally known as the Mexican Farm Labor Program, ended in 1964.

campesino: Spanish for farm worker or peasant

Chicano/Chicana: a man or woman of Mexican origin or descent

collective bargaining: a meeting of employee and employer representatives during which both sides negotiate wages and other conditions of employment

communism: a political theory based on the social and economic beliefs that all citizens should be treated equally and all wealth should be shared

corrido: a traditional Mexican folksong or ballad that tells a story, often about struggle against oppression and injustice

credit union: a nonprofit-making money cooperative whose members can borrow at low interest rates

deport: force a person to leave a country

disability insurance: income protection awarded to individuals who have suffered injuries directly related to their work

emeritus: a term indicating an unpaid position of honor that frees the individual from daily responsibilities usually associated with the title

fast: to abstain from all or some kinds of food or drink, often as a form of protest or in religious observance

feminist: someone who believes in social, economic, and political equality for women

Great Depression: the severe worldwide economic recession that lasted from 1929 to 1939. The depression forced the closure of businesses around the world, leaving millions of people out of work.

grassroots: the idea of building an organization with ordinary people regarded as the main body of its membership

gringo: non-Mexican whites

indefatigable: persisting tirelessly

indigenous: native to a region

LGBT: individuals who identify their sex or gender as other than traditionally heterosexual male or female

lobbying: when groups or individuals work to persuade lawmakers and/or government officials to alter government decisions, including laws and rules, in their favor or on behalf of a cause

loophole: an inadequacy in the law or a set of rules

machete: a broad, heavy knife used primarily as a tool for cutting sugarcane and underbrush

machismo: strong or aggressive masculine pride based on the belief that men are superior to women

mimeograph: a duplicating machine that produces copies by pressing ink through a stencil

pensions: money paid to someone after they have retired

pesticides: chemicals sprayed on crops to boost their growth or kill invading insects and plant diseases

picket: someone who protests publicly

picket lines: rows of people posted for a demonstration or protest

Presidential Medal of Freedom: the highest national civilian honor presented to individuals who have contributed to the security or national interests of the United States, to world peace, or to cultural or other significant public or private endeavors

racism: targeting or attributing characteristics to someone because of their race

sexism: prejudice against women; thinking by males that they are inherently better than women

sit-in: a form of protest in which a group of people occupy a place, sitting on seats or the floor and refusing to leave until their demands are met

strike: a work stoppage by a group of workers to protest demands against an act or condition created by an employer

strikebreaker: a person who works or is employed in place of others who are on strike, thereby making the strike ineffectual. Also referred to as a scab worker.

union: an organization of workers who call for better wages and working conditions as one voice

welfare: aid in the form of money or basic necessities

zoot suit: fashion during the 1940s that was popular among Chicano, African American, Filipino, and Italian males and sported high-waisted, wide-legged and tight-cuffed trousers and a long coat with wide lapels and wide padded shoulders

Notes

Chapter 1. Harvesting the Fruits of Labor

1. "Obama Honors Medal of Freedom Recipients," May 29, 2012, video, Dolores Huerta Foundation, http://doloreshuerta.org/video-president-obama -honors-the-presidential-medal-of-freedom-recipients (accessed May 1, 2016).

2. Matt Compton, "President Obama Awards Medal of Freedom," The White House, President Barack Obama, May 29, 2012, obamawhitehouse .archives.gov/blog/2012/05/29/president-obama-awards-medal-freedom -dolores-huerta.org.

Chapter 2. Tilling the Soil

1. William J. Clinton, "Remarks on Presenting the Eleanor Roosevelt Award for Human Rights," December 6, 1999, *Weekly Compilation of Presidential Documents* (Washington, DC: Office of the Federal Register, National Archives and Records Administration, December 13, 1999), vol. 35, no. 49, 2521.

2. Eric Schlosser, "In the Strawberry Fields," *The Atlantic,* November 1995, 80–108, http://www.theatlantic.com/magazine/archive/1995/11/in-the -strawberry-fields/305754 (accessed February 18, 2004).

3. Dolores Huerta, interview with Studs Terkel, Studs Terkel Radio Archive, 1975, studsterkel.wfmt.com/blog/tag/doloreshuerta. Also available at facingfreedom.org/node1329.

4. Ibid.

5. "Interview with Dolores Huerta, Community Leader and Activist," *Teaching to Change LA* 4, no. 2 (2003–4), www.tcla/gseis.ucla.edu/equalterms/ dialogue/2/huerta.html. In Mario T. García, ed., *A Dolores Huerta Reader* (Albuquerque: University of New Mexico Press, 2008), 348.

6. Dolores Huerta, interview with Studs Terkel.

7. Ibid.

8. Janet Morey and Wendy Dunn, *Famous Mexican Americans* (London: Puffin Books, 1997), 41.

9. Ibid.

Chapter 3. Fertilizing the Soil

1. Todd Eisenstadt, "41 Years in the Grass Roots Organizer Fred Ross, 76, Still Has Work to Do," *Chicago Tribune*, July 14, 1987, www.articles.chicagotribune .com/1987-07-14/features/8702210433_1_ross-son-united-farm-worker -cesar-chavez.

2. Dolores Huerta, "Dolores Huerta Talks about Republicans, César, Her Children, and Her Home Town," *Regeneracíon* 2, no. 4 (1975): 20.

3. Puffin/Nation Prize for Creative Citizenship, "Dolores Huerta: 2002 Recipient," The Puffin Foundation, Ltd. and The Nation Institute, http://www .nationinstitute.org/puffinnation/huerta.html (accessed February 24, 2004).

4. Daniel Rothenberg, *With These Hands: The Hidden World of Migrant Farmworkers Today* (Boston: Houghton Mifflin Harcourt, 1998), 242.

5. Jacques E. Levy, *César Chávez: Autobiography of La Causa* (New York: W. W. Norton & Company, 1975) 145.

Chapter 4. Planting the Seeds

1. Daniel Rothenberg, *With These Hands*, 242.

2. National Farm Workers Association—Organizational Meeting, September 30, 1962, Minutes, NFWA Collection, Series III, General Topics, 1960–1967, box 5, Archives of Labor and Urban Affairs, Walter P. Reuther Library, Wayne State University, Detroit, Michigan, reuther.wayne.edu/files/LR000221 _NFW.pdf. In Jacques E. Levy, *César Chávez*, 175.

3. Dolores Huerta, "Dolores Huerta Talks about Republicans, César, Children, and Her Home Town," 21.

4. Julie Felner, "Woman of the Year: Dolores Huerta, For a Lifetime of Labor Championing the Rights of Farmworkers," *Ms.* magazine, January/February 1998, 3. In García, *A Dolores Huerta Reader*, 133–39.

5. Dolores Huerta, "Dolores Huerta Talks about Republicans, César, Children, and Her Home Town," 21.

6. Ibid.

7. Levy, *César Chávez*, xxiii.

Chapter 5. Tending the Soil

1. Richard Griswold del Castillo and Richard A. Garcia, *César Chávez: A Triumph of Spirit* (Norman: University of Oklahoma Press, 1995), 59.

2. Tia Tenopia, "Biography—Dolores Huerta, Labor Organizer," *Latinopia*, March 6, 2010, http://www.latinopia.com/latino-history/dolores-huerta (accessed May 3, 2016).

3. Gloria Steinem, interview with author, March 3, 2016.

4. Ibid.

5. Margaret Eleanor Rose, "Women in the United Farm Workers: A Study of Chicana and Mexicana Participation in a Labor Union, 1950 to 1980" (PhD diss., University of California at Los Angeles, 1988), 80.

6. Julie Felner, "Woman of the Year: Dolores Huerta, For a Lifetime of Labor Championing the Rights of Farmworkers," 3.

7. Ibid.

8. Inga Kim, "The History of the UFW: Conditions of Farm Workers and Their Work," United Farm Workers, www.ufw.org/the-rise-of-the-ufw/. Also in David Oddo, "Farm Worker Conditions," National Farm Worker Ministry, www.nfwm.org/tag/worker-conditions/.

9. Kathy Murguía and Abby Rivera, "De Colores," *The UFW: Songs and Stories Sung and Told by UFW Volunteers,* Farmworker Movement Documentation Project, (San Diego: University of California, San Diego, 2004) 6–7, https://libraries.ucsd.edu/farmworkermovement/media/Scott /INTRODUCTIONTOSONGSANDCOMMENTARY(FINAL) (accessed May 18, 2016).

Chapter 6. Thinning the Shoots

1. Dolores Huerta, interview with Studs Terkel.

2. *The Fight in the Fields: César Chávez and the Farmworkers' Struggle,* documentary, directed by Rick Tejada-Flores and Ray Telles (Independent Television Service and Paradigm Productions, Inc., 1997), www.paradigmproductions.org/paradigm.html. In Susan Ferris and Ricardo Sandoval, *The Fight in the Fields: César Chávez and the Farmworkers' Movement,* edited by Diana Hembree (Boston: Houghton Mifflin Harcourt, 1997).

3. Rafaela G. Castro, *Dictionary of Chicano Folklore* (Santa Barbara, CA: ABC-CLIO, 2000), 138.

4. Ibid.

5. Judith Coburn, "Dolores Huerta: La Pasionaria of the Farmworkers," *Ms.* magazine, February 2004, 11. In García, *A Dolores Huerta Reader*, 105–114.

6. Dolores Huerta, "Dolores Huerta Talks about Republicans, César, Children, and Her Home Town," 22.

7. "The History of Si Se Puede," United Farm Workers, http://www.ufw .org/research/history/history-si-se-puede/ (accessed May 6, 2016).

8. Dolores Huerta, interview with Studs Terkel.

9. Julie Felner, "Woman of the Year: Dolores Huerta, For a Lifetime of Labor Championing the Rights of Farmworkers," 3.

10. Octavio I. Romano-V., "Dolores Huerta," *TQS NEWS: A Contemporary Newsletter of Eclectic Chicano Thought* (Berkeley: TQS Publications, 1995), http:// web.mit.edu/21f.714/www/hispanos/huerta.html (accessed June 12, 2016).

11. Barbara Baer, "Stopping Traffic: One Woman's Cause," *The Progressive* 39, no. 9 (September 1975): 39. In García, *A Dolores Huerta Reader*, 97–104.

12. Julie Felner, "Woman of the Year: Dolores Huerta, For a Lifetime of Labor Championing the Rights of Farmworkers," 3.

13. Barbara Baer, "Stopping Traffic: One Woman's Cause," 38.

14. Ibid.

15. Barbara Baer and Glenna Matthews, "'You Find a Way': The Women of the Boycott," *The Nation*, February 23, 1974, 233. In García, *A Dolores Huerta Reader*, 79–92.

16. Dolores Huerta, interview with Tavis Smiley, National Public Radio, May 5, 2003, transcript from www.lexisnexis@prod.lexisnexis.com (accessed April 12, 2004).

Chapter 7. Weeding the Fields

1. Eduardo Porter, "Moving On from Farm and Factory," Economic Scene, *New York Times*, B1, April 27, 2016.

2. Gaylynn Burroughs, "Dolores Huerta: Still Fighting for Farmworkers' Rights," *Ms.* magazine blog, May 4, 2015, http://msmagazine.com/blog/2015 /05/04/dolores-huerta-still-fighting-for-farmworkers-rights/ (accessed February 22, 2016).

3. Dolores Huerta, interview with Studs Terkel.

4. Ibid.

5. El Teatro Campesino, "Our History," elteatrocampesino.com/our -history/ (accessed June 10, 2016).

6. Lu Herrera, "For the Sake of Good," *Hispanic* 16, no. 5 (May 2003): 29.

7. Julie Felner, "Woman of the Year: Dolores Huerta, For a Lifetime of Labor Championing the Rights of Farmworkers," 3.

8. Sonia Benson, "Dolores Huerta," in *Hispanic Almanac: A Reference Work on Hispanics in the United States,* edited by Sonia Benson and Nicholas Kanellos, (Farmington Hills, MI: Gale, 2003), go.galegroup.com/ps/i.do?p=suic &a=bulldogs&sid=SUICRxid=292/eb12.

Chapter 8. Spreading More Seeds

1. Feminist Majority Foundation, "About Us," www.feminist.org/welcome /index.html (accessed May 11, 2016).

2. Feminist Majority Foundation, "Feminist Chronicles-1987," www .feminist.org/research/chronicles/fc1987.html (accessed May 29, 2016).

3. Joyce Maupin, "Labor Heroines," *Union WAGE (Women's Alliance to Gain Equality),* July–August 1974, 6. Also published as *Labor Heroines: The Women Who Led the Struggle* (Berkeley: Union WAGE, 1974), Labor Archives and Research Center, J. Paul Leonard Library, San Francisco State University, San Francisco, CA, collection larcms.0004, accession 1986/022.

4. Ibid.

5. Richard Griswold del Castillo and Richard Garcia, *César Chávez: A Triumph of Spirit,* xiii–xi.

6. Ibid, 72.

7. Susan Ferris and Ricardo Sandoval, *The Fight in the Fields: César Chávez and the Farmworkers Movement.*

8. Ibid, 274.

9. *Hispanic,* August 1996.

10. Julie Felner, "Woman of the Year: Dolores Huerta, For a Lifetime of Labor Championing the Rights of Farmworkers," 3.

11. Lu Herrera, "For the Sake of Good," 29.

12. Juliana Barbassa, "Dolores Huerta Starts Foundation to Promote Organizing," *San Francisco Chronicle,* August 18, 2003.

Chapter 9. Another Harvest

1. National Women's History Project, "Dolores Huerta: Labor Leader with a Passion for Justice," www.nwhp.org//?s=Dolores+Huerta&x=8&y=8.

2. Lu Herrera, "For the Sake of Good," 28.

3. Roque Planas, "The Most Latino Congress Ever Is Coming in 2015," HuffPost, November 5, 2014, www.huffingtonpost.com/2014/11/05/latinos-in -congress_n_6111410.html (accessed June 21, 2016).

4. Richard Griswold del Castillo and Richard A. García, *César Chávez: A Triumph of Spirit,* 75.

Bibliography

Books

Benson, Sonia, and Nicholas Kanellos, eds. *Hispanic Almanac: A Reference Work on Hispanics in the United States.* Farmington Hills, MI: Gale, 2003.

Castro, Rafaela G. *Dictionary of Chicano Folklore.* Santa Barbara, CA: ABC-CLIO, 2000.

Ferris, Susan, and Ricardo Sandoval. Edited by Diana Hembree. *The Fight in the Fields: César Chávez and the Farmworkers' Movement.* Boston: Houghton Mifflin Harcourt, 1997.

García, Mario T., ed. *A Dolores Huerta Reader.* Albuquerque: University of New Mexico Press, 2008.

Gore Schiff, Karenna. *Lighting the Way: Nine Women Who Changed Modern America.* New York, Miramax Books, 2006.

Griswold del Castillo, Richard, and Richard A. Garcia. *César Chávez: A Triumph of Spirit.* Norman: University of Oklahoma Press, 1995.

Levy, Jacques E. *César Chávez: Autobiography of La Causa.* New York: W. W. Norton & Company, 1975.

Morey, Janet, and Wendy Dunn. *Famous Mexican Americans.* London: Puffin Books, 1997.

Rothenberg, Daniel. *With These Hands: The Hidden World of Migrant Farmworkers Today.* Boston: Houghton Mifflin Harcourt, 1998.

Articles

Baer, Barbara. "Stopping Traffic: One Woman's Cause." *The Progressive* 39, no. 9 (September 1975): 38–40.

Baer, Barbara, and Glenna Matthews. "'You Find a Way': The Women of the Boycott." *The Nation,* February 23, 1974, 232–38.

Barbassa, Juliana. "Dolores Huerta Starts Foundation to Promote Organizing." *San Francisco Chronicle,* August 18, 2003.

Burroughs, Gaylynn. "Dolores Huerta: Still Fighting for Farmworkers' Rights." *Ms.* magazine blog, May 4, 2015. http://msmagazine.com/blog/2015/05/04/dolores-huerta-still-fighting-for-farmworkers-rights/.

Coburn, Judith. "Dolores Huerta: La Pasionaria of the Farmworkers." *Ms.* magazine, February 2004.

Compton, Matt. "President Obama Awards Medal of Freedom." The White House, President Barack Obama, May 29, 2012. obamawhitehouse.archives.gov/blog/2012/05/29/president-obama-awards-medal-freedom-dolores-huerta.org.

Eisenstadt, Todd. "41 Years in the Grass Roots Organizer Fred Ross, 76, Still Has Work to Do." *Chicago Tribune,* July 14, 1987. www.articles.chicagotribune.com/1987-07-14/features/8702210433_1_ross-son-united-farm-worker-cesar-chavez.

Felner, Julie. "Woman of the Year: Dolores Huerta, For a Lifetime of Labor Championing the Rights of Farmworkers." *Ms.* magazine, January/February 1998.

Herrera, Lu. "For the Sake of Good." *Hispanic* 16, no. 5 (2003): 28–29.

Huerta, Dolores. "Dolores Huerta Talks about Republicans, César, Her Children, and Her Home Town." *Regeneración* 2, no. 4 (1975): 20–24.

Kim, Inga. "The History of the UFW: Conditions of Farm Workers and Their Work." United Farm Workers. www.ufw.org/the-rise-of-the-ufw/.

Maupin, Joyce. "Labor Heroines." *Union WAGE (Women's Alliance to Gain Equality),* July–August 1974, 6. Also published as *Labor Heroines: The Women Who Led the Struggle.* Berkeley, Union WAGE, 1974. Labor Archives and Research Center, J. Paul Leonard Library, San Francisco State University, San Francisco, CA, collection larcms.0004, accession 1986/022.

Murguía, Kathy, and Abby Rivera. "De Colores." *The UFW: Songs and Stories Sung and Told by UFW Volunteers.* Farmworker Movement Documentation Project, San Diego, University of California at San Diego, 2004. https://libraries.ucsd.edu/farmworkermovement/media/Scott/INTRODUCTIONTOSONGSANDCOMMENTARY(FINAL) (accessed May 18, 2016).

Oddo, David. "Farm Worker Conditions." National Farm Worker Ministry. www.nfwm.org/tag/worker-conditions/.

Planas, Roque. "The Most Latino Congress Ever Is Coming in 2015." Huff-Post, November 5, 2014. www.huffingtonpost.com/2014/11/05/latinos-in-congress_n_6111410.html (accessed June 21, 2016).

Porter, Eduardo. "Moving On from Farm and Factory." Economic Scene. *New York Times,* B1, April 27, 2016.

Romano-V., Octavio I. "Dolores Huerta." *TQS NEWS: A Contemporary News-letter of Eclectic Chicano Thought.* Berkeley, TQS Publications, 1995. http: //web.mit.edu/21f.714/www/hispanos/huerta.html (accessed June 12, 2016).

Schlosser, Eric. "In the Strawberry Fields." *The Atlantic,* November 1995, 80–108. http://www.theatlantic.com/magazine/archive/1995/11/in-the-strawberry -fields/305754 (accessed February 18, 2004).

Tenopia, Tia. "Biography—Dolores Huerta, Labor Organizer." *Latinopia,* March 6, 2010. http://www.latinopia.com/latino-history/dolores-huerta.

Miscellaneous Publications

Clinton, William J. "Remarks on Presenting the Eleanor Roosevelt Award for Human Rights." December 6, 1999. *Weekly Compilation of Presidential Documents.* Washington, DC, Office of the Federal Register, National Archives and Records Administration, December 13, 1999, vol. 35, no. 49, 2521.

National Farm Workers Association—Organizational Meeting, September 30, 1962, Minutes. NFWA Collection, Series III, General Topics, 1960–1967, box 5. Archives of Labor and Urban Affairs, Walter P. Reuther Library, Wayne State University, Detroit, Michigan. reuther.wayne.edu/files /LR000221_NFW.pdf.

Petersen, Jan, and Terry Scott, eds. *The UFW: Songs and Stories Sung and Told by UFW Volunteers.* Pdf. Farmworker Movement Documentation Project. 2004.

Puffin/Nation Prize for Creative Citizenship. "Dolores Huerta: 2002 Recipient." The Puffin Foundation, Ltd. and The Nation Institute. http://www .nationinstitute.org/puffinnation/huerta.html (accessed February 24, 2004).

Rose, Margaret Eleanor. "Women in the United Farm Workers: A Study of Chicana and Mexicana Participation in a Labor Union, 1950–1980." Dissertation, 1988. University of California at Los Angeles.

Films and Videos

Brothers on the Line. Documentary. Directed by Alexander (Sasha) Reuther. Produced by Alexander Reuther and Nancy Roth, 2012. www .brothersontheline.com.

Dolores. Documentary. Directed by Peter Bratt. Produced by Carlos Santana, 2018. www.doloresthemovie.com.

"Obama Honors Medal of Freedom Recipients." May 29, 2012. Dolores Huerta Foundation. htp://doloreshuerta.org/video-president-obama-honors-the -presidential-medal-of-freedom-recipients (accessed May 1, 2016).

Song for César, the Movement and the Music. Documentary. Directed by Andres Alegria and Abel Sanchez. San Francisco, CA: Song for César, KPIX-TV (archives), KOED-TV (archives), and San Francisco Bay Area Television Archives, 2018. www.the-song.html.

The Fight in the Fields: César Chávez and the Farmworkers' Struggle. Documentary. Directed by Rick Tejada-Flores and Ray Telles. Produced by Independent Television Service and Paradigm Productions, Inc., 1997. www.paradigmproductions.org/paradigm.html.

Interviews

Dolores Huerta. Interview with Studs Terkel, 1975. Studs Terkel Radio Archive. studsterkel.wfmt.com/blog/tag/doloreshuerta. Also available at facingfreedom.org/node1329.

Dolores Huerta. Interview with Tavis Smiley. National Public Radio, May 5, 2003. lexisnexis@prod.lexisnexis.com. (accessed April 12, 2004).

Gloria Steinem. Interview with author, March 3, 2016.

Websites

El Teatro Campesino, elteatrocampesino.com.

Farmworker Movement Documentation Project. UC San Diego Library, University of California, San Diego. www.libraries.ucsd.edu /farmworkermovement/.

Feminist Majority Foundation, www.feminist.org.

National Farms Workers Ministry, www.nfwm.org.

National Women's History Project, www.nwhp.org.

United Farm Workers, www.ufw.org.